Phil Maggitti

Pugs

Everything about Purchase, Care, Nutrition,
Breeding, Behavior, and Training
with 43 color photographs;

Drawings by Michele Earle-Bridges

BARRON'S

Contents

*"They all had a free and glorious life,
and your own is sweetened by the
certainty you have brought only
unconfined delight to a creature
whose existence wags and spins on
your love and approval."*
  –John Osborne, *The Spectator,*
  7 May 1994

Preface

When I began this book, we had four pug dogs. Last Halloween, about three months before the manuscript was due, we took one of those dogs, who belongs to friends of ours, to be bred. Exactly two months later, on December 30, what we sometimes referred to as the trick-or-treat litter was born.

There were six puppies in that litter. One of them, a boy named Hans, decided that conditions were precisely to his liking here in his ancestral home and that, if it was all the same to us, he would like to remain here to keep an eye on his mother and grand-mother. We agreed.

Growing your own is the surest way of acquiring a puppy about which you know all there possibly is to know. You have seen the puppy being born, in most cases. You have smiled as it scrimmaged with its littermates for a place in the food line. You have chuckled as it learned to walk, first crawling, then wobbling to its feet, standing, tottering, falling, righting itself, looking about uncertainly, and finally taking a few gravity-defying steps. You have laughed when, presented with a small dish of food as weaning was begun, the puppy waded through it, fell into it, and wound up with more food on the out-side of its body than on the inside. You have watched as its teeth and its personality emerged. You have seen it when it was sleeping. You have known when it was awake. You have begun to house-train it, and you have taken it to the veterinarian for its shots. Next to that puppy's mother and its littermates, you are more intimately acquainted with it than is anyone else in the world.

Few people get to select a puppy, much less an adult dog, in this fashion; but wherever they acquire puppies, new owners should try to learn as much about them as they possibly can. A good deal of that information will be supplied by the person from whom one acquires a puppy. Breeders, obviously, are in the best position to answer all the questions a prospective owner might have. Another excellent source of information, if I might make bold to suggest, is the book you are holding. Its eleven chapters were designed to make living with a pug more easy, enjoyable, and rewarding. Every chapter contains information that will help new pug owners— and perhaps a few older ones—to understand their pugs more thoroughly and to care for them more efficiently.

"A Few Words about Pug History" discusses the pug's origin and traces some of the steps in the campaign with which it conquered the world. "A Pug of Your Own" will help readers decide whether they should get a male or a female, where they might acquire a pug, when and why they should have that pug altered, how to determine if a puppy is healthy, and more. "Life with a Pug" contains a shopping list for new owners, provides hints about pug-proofing a house, explains the importance of a crate, reveals the secret of house-training (knowing when your dog has to go outside before he or she does), and tells owners how to introduce a collar, harness, children, and other pets to a pug.

"Routine Care and Grooming" includes—among other things—advice regarding bathing, brushing, nail clipping, ear cleaning, and keeping a pug's wrinkles wrinkle-free. "The Well-fed Pug" tells how to decipher a dog-food label, how to navigate through the pet-food aisles of a supermarket or feed store, how much and how often to feed a pug, and how to compare the merits of the various kinds of dog food available: dry, semi-moist, canned, generic, private label, regular, or superpremium. "The Healthy Pug" contains a veterinary checklist to help the new owner spot signs of trouble. It also explains the importance of vaccinations, how to wage war on fleas, how to medicate and feed a sick pug, and which congenital problems are most common to pugs.

"Understanding Your Pug" contains anecdotes and observations that provide insights into the pug's delightful character. "Two for the Shows" explains how to locate, enter, prepare for, and survive your first and subsequent dog shows. The hints provided and the lessons described in "Obedience Training" will help to make your pug well mannered.

"Should You Breed Your Pug?" begins by discussing the reasons why most persons should not and then, for the benefit of the few people who qualify or think they qualify as prospective pug parents, goes on to discuss strategies for producing the best pug puppy. "Whelping and Raising Puppies" is a thorough, recently reverified primer on caring for a mother and babies.

Short of raising a puppy of your own, *The Pug Dog: A Complete Pet Owner's Manual* is the best way of acquiring the knowledge that will help you to choose and care for a pug. What's more, reading a book is a lot less work.

Phil Maggitti

A Few Words About Pug History

The first recorded appearance of the word *pug* in the English language occurred in 1566. Pug was a term of endearment then applied to persons but rarely to animals. By 1600 pug had acquired two additional meanings: courtesan and bargeman. These would appear to be strange bedfellows, linguistically at least, but pug did not stop there in its acquisition of new meanings. By 1664 pug also meant demon, imp, sprite, monkey, and ape.

The preceding definitions of pug all predated the arrival of the pug dog in England, which glorious event occurred in November 1688 when the Dutch prince William III of Orange landed at Torbay in South Devonshire with his wife, the English Princess Mary, to ascend the English throne. Although William never became popular in England, his pugs and their descendants did; and by the middle of the next century, according to *The Oxford English Dictionary* (OED), pug had come to mean "a dwarf breed of dog resembling a bull-dog in miniature." The OED also added that the pug "on account of its affectionate nature [was] much kept as a pet." So much so that in 1749 David Garrick, the English actor and theatrical manager, wrote, "A fine lady . . . keeps a Pug-dog and hates the Parsons."

Monkeying Around with Definitions

Some disagreement exists regarding the manner in which pug came to be applied to these endearing, impish, spritelike, solid-as-a-barge, sometimes demonic little monkeys that were great favorites at court. Many observers believe that pug first was applied to monkeys, and, after certain facial resemblances between monkeys and the little dogs with the curly tails had been noted, the word was applied to the dogs, too. (This application was reported as early as 1731 in England.) Persons subscribing to this theory point out that pugs were called pug dogs originally to distinguish them from pug monkeys.

Other observers wrote that pug was derived from the Latin *pugnus*, meaning fist, because to some people the pug's profile resembled a clenched fist. Still others believe pug is a corruption of Puck, the mischievous fairy in Shakespeare's *A Midsummer Night's Dream*. The puckish nature of the pug would seem to support this theory, but the OED does not. After acknowledging that pug "agrees completely in sense with Puck," the OED cautions that pug "is not easily accounted for as a mere phoenetic variant" of Puck.

Like so many questions regarding animal history, the matter of how the pug got its name eventually devolves to a no-one-can-be-certain resolution. Our money is on the borrowed-from-the-monkey name theory; but before we leave this question, we should point out that pug also has been applied to lambs, hares, squirrels, ferrets, salmon, moths, small locomotives, fox, trout, clay, and the footprints of any beast.

Dutch Masters and Mistresses

Although no one knows for certain when or where the pug arrived in Europe, the Dutch are usually credited with being the agents of the pug's importation. Called the Mopshond, a Dutch word for *grumble*, the pug was greatly favored by Dutch ladies, who kept warm in their large, unheated houses, we are told, by placing a pug or two on their laps.

By the time William III and his pugs arrived in England, the pug had been anointed the official dog of the House of Orange in the Netherlands. The pug's elevation occurred after a pug named Pompey had saved the life of William III's grandfather, Prince William the Silent. The governor of Holland and a fancier of pugs, William the Silent left the Netherlands for Germany in 1567 after Philip II of Spain had sent an army to Holland to put down an armed revolt that had arisen the year before. Unwilling to remain silent forever, William led a counteroffensive against the Spanish army in 1572. One night during that campaign, as William lay sleeping in his tent at Hermigny, assassins approached. Pompey began barking and scratching in an attempt to warn his master. Finally, he leapt upon William's face to alert him to the approaching danger.

Continental Favorites

Pugs were royal favorites in France as well as England, and by the time pugs arrived in England in the latter part of the seventeenth century, they also had emigrated to France. Perhaps the best-known pug fancier in France was Josephine, wife of the emperor, Napoleon. Josephine's pug, Fortune, bit Napoleon on the leg when he was climbing into bed on Napoleon and Josephine's wedding night. Fortune survived that encounter, but he did not survive a challenge to the cook's English bulldog. Following his misfortune, the pugnacious little dog was replaced by another pug named Fortune; when the unfortunate Josephine was imprisoned at Les Carmes, Napoleon sent love notes to her hidden in Fortune II's collar.

The pug was well-known in Italy and Spain during the eighteenth century. In 1789 a Mrs. Piozzi wrote in her journal, "The little pug dog or Dutch mastiff has quitted London for Padua, I perceive. Every carriage I meet here has a pug in it."

A painting by Goya places the pug, or *Dogullo* as it was called, in Spain by 1785; and the use of the word *Mopsorden* (Order of the Pug) by Masons in Germany, who were excommunicated by the Pope in 1736, serves to date the pug in that country.

The word pug began life in the middle of the sixteenth century as a term of endearment applied mostly to people. By the early seventeenth century pug also meant courtesan or bargeman. Can you guess which these are?

7

Be it ever so humble or grand, a pug's home is his castle.

The Pug Dog's Origin

Questions about the pug's origin, like questions about the derivation of its name, elicit more nobody-knows-for-certain answers. Most authorities agree, however, that the pug is an Oriental breed, whose common ancestors are the Pekingese and the lion dog (the ancestor of today's Shih Tzu), and whose country of origin is China. Estimates of the time at which the pug originated are varied: before 400 B.C., says one observer; in 600 B.C., says another; over 1,800 years ago, says a third. This uncertainty is occasioned in no small part by the Emperor Chin Shih, who destroyed all records, scrolls, and art relating to the pug sometime during his dynasty, which lasted from 255 to 205 B.C.

As others would do who would know and love the pug in later centuries, the Chinese had several names for pugs, including Foo or Fu dog, Lo-Chiang-Sze, Lo-Chiang, Pia dog, and Hand dog. The Chinese also were known to send animals as gifts to important individuals in Korea and Japan. Thus, the pug arrived in those countries during the seventh and eighth centuries.

In vogue, now as then, a modern-day black pug strikes a pose in front of a reproduction of an ancient Chinese Foo dog statue.

The pug combines a jolly disposition with a face that looks as if it has just been the recipient of bad news.

The Black Pug

Black pugs, at least one researcher believes, were developed in Japan in the late ninth or early tenth centuries. From there the black pugs' spread to other parts of the world mirrored that of their fawn relatives. Some of the earliest black pugs and, hence, some of the earliest fawn pugs—and even the occasional modern-day fawn pug, if the truth be known—were decorated with patches of white in their coats.

The Pug in America

The first pugs imported to the United States arrived shortly after the Civil War. The breed was accepted by the American Kennel Club in 1885, but after a promising start in this country pugs were overshadowed by longer-coated toy breeds such as the Pekingese and the Pomeranian. From 1900 to 1920 only a handful of breeders were working with pugs, and many shows drew no pug entry at all.

The first pug dog club in this country was started in 1931, but that club did not last much past its first show, which was held in 1937. In the early 1950s the Pug Dog Club of America, the parent club of the breed, was founded. Today the pug ranks in the mid-twenties among the 136 breeds recognized by the American Kennel Club.

Though not seen as frequently as their fawn relatives, black pugs are equally charming and companionable.

9

A Pug of Your Own

There are few more pleasurable occasions in life than the day on which you go to pick out a dog, but if the decision to acquire a dog is to be a wise and lasting one, there are several questions you must answer beforehand. Where is the best place to acquire a dog—from a breeder, a pet shop, or an animal shelter? How much should you expect to pay? How can you tell if the dog you like is healthy and has a good personality? Do you want a male or female? A puppy, an adolescent, or an adult? A fawn pug or a black one? Should you get one dog or two?

Male or Female?

Some people, because of personal inclination or prior experience, prefer the companionship of either male or female dogs; but given love, a supply of things to chew, and a place on the bed at night, either sex will make a fine companion. The cost of spaying a female pug is $30 or so more than the cost of neutering a male. Otherwise there is no difference in the expense associated with housing an altered male or female—and no difference in the amount of care each requires.

Why You Should Alter Your Pug

Altered dogs make more civilized companions. Unaltered males are wont to lift their legs to anoint vertical objects with urine as a means of marking territory and attracting females. Unaltered males also are inclined to make sexual advances to your guests' legs and to regard any other dog as a potential mate or sparring partner.

Most unaltered females come into season (or heat) twice a year. This condition is accompanied by vulvar swelling, blood spots on the rugs, and, quite frequently, unannounced visits from neighborhood dogs who leave their calling cards in the herb garden. A heat lasts 21 days, on average, but they will be among the longest 21 days you ever endure.

There are socially responsible reasons for altering your pug, too. Although breeding a handsome, loving, well-mannered dog can provide joy, satisfaction, and the feeling of achievement that accompanies any creative activity, there is enormous responsibility incurred when that activity involves creating a life. Too many puppies are produced by irresponsible people who are looking to feed their competitive egos, turn a quick profit, or let their children observe the miracle of birth. Better they should take their children to an animal shelter and let them observe the underside of that miracle: the euthanasia of homeless dogs, who invariably go to meet the needle with their tails wagging. There is no more gut-wrenching sight in all the negotiations between animals and humans.

With millions of healthy dogs being destroyed annually for want of responsible owners, the decision to bring more puppies into the world is not one to be made lightly. For all but a few people it is not one that should be made at all. The pet overpopulation problem cannot be solved by the unrestricted breeding of puppies. The number of dogs killed in shelters each year argues for restraint and common sense on the part of humans, especially those who call themselves animal lovers.

When to Alter Your Pug

Most veterinarians recommend that females be spayed when they are about six months old and that males be neutered when they are seven to ten months old. At these ages sexual development is nearly complete, but undesirable traits—urine marking by male dogs, for example—have not become habits.

Puppy, Adolescent, or Adult

If pug puppies were more appealing, they would be illegal. What they lack in brainpower they make up for in curiosity. What they lack in experience they make up for in exuberance. They stomp joyfully through their food bowls and their days, tails wagging, heads lolling, eyes shining, bellies and hearts overflowing.

Pug puppies do not consider anyone a stranger and with luck they never will. They stir us to laughter, reduce us to baby talk, and summon from us a tenderness concealed beneath the armor we wear in our daily confrontations with life. Small wonder that long-term relationships between pugs and their owners often begin with a terminal case of puppy love.

The adolescent pug, while slightly less manic, is just as appealing as his neonate self. We acquired our first pug, a neutered fawn boy named Percy, when he was nine months old. If he had better moves as a puppy, I am sorry I missed them.

Percy was chauffeured from Florida to Pennsylvania in late January by a handler returning from the Florida circuit. We arrived at the handler's house with a crate in the back of our Geo Storm hatchback. After we had put

Percy into the crate, my wife returned to the house to get her purse. I said idly, "Well, Percy, how's it going?" and the little chap nearly came out of his skin. He began to bark, whoop, and whine and hop up and down, pawing at the bars of the crate until I thought he was going to declaw himself. I opened the crate and he fairly leaped into my arms, still in the throes of a ten-plus turn-on because I had known his name.

When my wife returned to the car, I returned Percy to his crate. He was still so excited that he peed all over the cage before we got to the end of the driveway and was obliged to sit on my lap the rest of the way home. If a puppy could top that whirling dervish performance, I would like to make that puppy's acquaintance.

The adult pug: If the adolescent pug is not much different from a puppy, an adult is not much different from an adolescent. Indeed, it is difficult to determine where adolescence leaves off and adulthood begins with pugs. We have two 23-month-old females in the house that show no signs of approaching or even contemplating adulthood. They chase each other about the yard as they have since they were old enough to run, and Ella, the

Although they yield to no other breed in the venerable art of lap sitting, pugs are also happy to act as escorts should their owners feel the need to go power walking.

slower of the two, still grabs Patty by the tail to make sure she does not get away. If this book finds enough readers to merit additional printings, I am sure Ella still will be hitching a ride on Patty's tail as I make revisions to this copy, and I still will be hoping that she and Patty never grow up.

The black pug listens attentively while the fawn pug holds forth.

Fawn or Black

A pug's physical characteristics are governed by genes—the coding units that transmit genetic instructions from an individual to his or her offspring. Genes, as you remember from high-school biology, are arranged in pairs on chromosomes, and each gene occupies a specific address (or site) on a chromosome. That address is called the gene's locus (plural, loci).

Each member of a pair of genes can occur in different forms, called alleles. At the color loci in a pug, for example, there can be an allele that tells the coat to be all black or an allele that tells the coat to be fawn with black ears and mask. The allele for black is dominant. Thus, a pug will be black if he inherits one black allele

and one fawn allele—or two black alleles. Consequently, there is only one or two allele's difference between a black and a fawn pug, and the choice between a black and a fawn is, essentially, a matter of aesthetics.

One Dog or Two

If you have no other pets and if your house is empty during the day, you should consider getting two pugs. If buying a second pug would tax your budget, adopt a dog—one that is roughly the same age and will grow up to be roughly the same size as the pug you are purchasing—from a local shelter. Not only will you double your pleasure by watching two dogs playing instead of one, but your dogs will be less apt to get bored or lonely if they have company when you are away. Of course, when you adopt a dog from a shelter, you should follow the same guidelines you would follow when purchasing one. (See "The Healthy Puppy," page 16.)

Many breeders of pedigreed dogs imply—and others assert—that one cannot have as much confidence in a shelter dog's personality as in a pure-bred's. That belief is rubbish. Because

A pug swat team at play. The rules for swat are simple: one pug takes an object in its mouth and starts running; the other pug tries to swat the object away.

they take in far more animals than they can place, most shelters screen their dogs thoroughly and euthanize any that are not sound physically or emotionally. Good breeders will keep their less-than-perfect puppies. Unscrupulous breeders will try to dump their bad stock on the first gullible buyer. Your chances of getting a nonquality dog from a shelter are no greater than they are of getting one from a breeder. Indeed, as Joe Stahlkuppe has observed in *Keeshonden,* another breed manual in this series, "For every responsible dog breeder who will help you find a good puppy there are several others to whom only your money is a motivation."

Show Dog or Pet

Unless you are planning to show and/or breed, you want a pet-quality pug. Pet quality—an unfortunate and snotty-sounding term—is used to designate dogs with some cosmetic liability that argues against their breeding or showing success. Pet-quality pugs generally have muzzles that are too pinched, noses that are too prominent, tails that are not as tightly curled as a show dog's, or some other "fault" or minor constellation of faults. None of these surface defects in any way detracts from the pug's sterling personality, for every pug is a quality dog at heart.

If you want to throw your hat, your pug, and your money into the show ring (see "Buying a Show Dog," page 17), make that desire clear to the breeder when you go to look at puppies. Many first-time dog owners who cared not a whit about showing when they brought their pups home suddenly become flushed with pride in their dogs and mistakenly assume they are show prospects simply because they are pedigreed. But pedigrees do not make show dogs. Indeed, most pedigreed dogs are not show quality—if

Life imitating artworks: two pugs decorating a coffee table.

The pug has its own motto: Multum in parvo, *a Latin phrase that means "a lot of dog in a small space."*

show quality means good enough to earn a championship.

Helpful hint: If, after buying a pug at a pet price, you are suddenly inspired to begin writing to show superintendents for premium lists, let the dog's breeder know what you are interested in doing. Then ask if you can take the dog to the breeder for an evaluation. If you bought your dog from a breeder who lives far away, ask a local breeder to evaluate your dog. An ounce of prevention can be worth a pound of disappointment in the show ring.

Where to Find a Pug

At a breeder's: A conscientious breeder who raises a few well-socialized litters a year is an excellent source for a pug. Such dedicated individuals may advertise in dog magazines, in the classified sections of newspapers, on bulletin boards in veterinary offices, in grooming shops and feed stores, and in *Pug Talk*, a publication no pug lover should be without (see "Periodicals," page 92). Prospective buyers also can meet pug breeders by visiting dog shows, which are advertised in newspapers, veterinarians' offices, dog magazines, and, occasionally, on television.

At a pet shop: Anyone who decides to buy a pug from a pet shop should ask the pet-shop owner for the name, address, and phone number of the dog's breeder. If the pet-shop owner is unwilling or unable to provide that information, the buyer should proceed with caution because he or she is proceeding with less information about the puppy than normally would be available if the puppy was being purchased directly from his breeder.

If the pet-shop owner provides the name and address of the puppy's breeder—and if that person lives nearby—the prospective customer would do well to visit the breeder to observe the conditions in which the puppy was raised. If the breeder lives far away, the prospective buyer should telephone to ask questions about the puppy that the pet-shop operator might not be able to answer: How many other puppies were in the litter? How old was the puppy when he left his mother? How many dogs does the breeder have? How many litters do those dogs produce in a year? How many different breeds of puppies does the breeder produce? Why does the breeder choose to sell to pet shops rather than directly to the public? In addition, the prospective buyer should call the humane association in the town where the breeder lives to ask if the breeder enjoys a good reputation in that community.

Recommending this sort of caution is not to insinuate that buying from a pet store is, per se, more risky than buying directly from a breeder. What is implied, however, is that the buyer should find out as much as possible about a pug's background no matter where that dog is acquired.

At an animal shelter: Difficult as it may be to believe, some people, through no fault whatsoever of their

This unfortunate pug in an animal shelter probably is thinking, "What did I do wrong?" But behind virtually every animal in a shelter there is some human who has done wrong.

pugs, do not get along with their dogs. In such rare circumstances the unworthy owner should return the pug to his breeder, who, of course, will take the dog back promptly, find him another, more suitable home, or keep the dog forever—as all decent breeders should do without fail or hesitation.

Nevertheless, some pugs do wind up in animal shelters with their tails tucked, as far as they can tuck their tails, between their legs. If you are willing to wait for a pug until one is surrendered at a shelter near you, present yourself at the shelter and ask to be put on its waiting list. No matter how long you have to wait for a pug to arrive at the shelter, your patience will be rewarded, and a special place at the table in pug-lover's heaven will be set for you.

At a breed rescue club: While you are visiting the shelter, ask if there are any pug rescue clubs in the area. Members of rescue clubs often cooperate with shelters by providing foster homes for lost, abandoned, or surrendered pugs, feeding and caring for them while trying to locate suitable new owners.

How Much is that Doggie?

The price of a pug is determined by age, quality, supply, demand, and geography. Very young pugs, 12 weeks old or so, are generally priced between $400 and $800, depending on the breeder's assessment of their potential. A $400 puppy, though his topline may not be correct and his tail may not have enough curl, will make a lovely companion if he is healthy and properly socialized. So will an $800 puppy, which has been priced higher because his breeder feels he has some show potential. Puppies with a lot of show potential—as much as this determination can be made at such a young age, which is not much at all—are not usually available because their breeders want to see

how they develop. (See "Buying a Show Dog," page 17.)

How Old is Old Enough?

Puppyhood is one of the special joys of dog owning. Dogs are dogs their entire lives, but they are puppies for only a few precious months. Thus, their new owners are eager to take their puppies home as soon as possible. Nevertheless, responsible breeders do not let puppies go until they are between ten and twelve weeks old. By that age a puppy has been weaned properly, has been eating solid food for several weeks, and has begun to make the transition to adulthood.

Puppies that are fewer than ten weeks old are still babies. Take them away from their mothers and their siblings at that age, and the stress of adjusting to new surroundings may cause them to become sick, to be difficult to house-train, or to nurse on blankets or sofa cushions—a habit they sometimes keep the rest of their lives. No matter how tempting a seven-week-old puppy might be, he will adjust better if he is allowed to remain in his original home until he is several weeks older.

Unfortunately, some breeders are eager to place puppies as quickly as possible, especially those breeders who have hordes of puppies underfoot. Do not let an irresponsible breeder talk you into taking a puppy that is too young.

The most difficult and important aspect of raising pugs is screening potential buyers. No breeder should sell a pug to anyone with whom she would not be willing to go home herself.

If pug puppies were any more appealing, they would be illegal.

The Healthy Puppy

A healthy puppy's eyes are bright, glistening, and clear. His nose is cool and slightly damp. His gums are neither pale nor inflamed. His ears are free of wax or dirt. His body is smooth, perhaps a little plump, but not too skinny. His coat is plush to the touch and free of bald patches, scabs, or tiny specks of black dirt. The area around his tail is free of dirt or discoloration.

A puppy with teary eyes may be in poor health—especially if his nose is dry or if it feels warm. Inflamed gums may indicate gingivitis; a puppy with pale gums may be anemic. If his ears are waxy inside, that simply may be a sign of neglect; but if they exhibit caked-on dirt, the puppy may have ear mites. If a puppy's ribs are sticking out or if he is pot-bellied, he may be undernourished or he may have worms. A puppy with a dull-looking coat or one dotted with scabs, tiny specks of dirt, or bald spots may have ringworm or fleas. A puppy with wet hindquarters may develop urine scalding; if they are dirty, he may have diarrhea. Both urine scalding and diarrhea are signs of potential poor health.

Basic Personality Tests

The basic personality test for puppies is simple: Any puppy that comes racing over to investigate you as soon as he sees you is a good bet to make a swell companion. If you desire a more discriminating test, simply wiggle a few fingers along the floor about six inches in front of the puppy, or wave a small toy back and forth about the same distance away. Does the puppy rush to investigate? Does he back away in fright? Or does he disappear behind the nearest chair?

Well-adjusted, healthy puppies are curious about fingers, toys, and any-

Pugs are instinctive cuddlers, and they believe that humans are never too young to learn the art of nearness.

thing else within sight that moves. Nervous or timid puppies, or those that are not feeling well, are more cautious. Poorly adjusted puppies take cover behind the nearest chair.

If you have other pets or children at home, the inquisitive, hey-look-me-over puppy is the best choice. The bashful puppy may well make a fine companion, too, but he may take longer to adjust; he is, perhaps, better left for experienced dog owners who are currently without pets or young children. And the little one behind the chair? Shy puppies need love also. Plenty of it. If you have no other pets or if you plan to acquire two puppies at once and have the time and patience required to nurture such a reluctant violet, God bless you. If not, perhaps the next person who comes along will be the right owner for this needful pup.

Although temperament is heritable to some degree, the way a puppy is raised is more important in shaping his personality. Pugs that are not handled often enough between the ages of three and twelve weeks are less likely to develop into well-adjusted family members than puppies who receive frequent handling and attention during that period. Therefore, it is well to ask how many litters a breeder produces each year and how many other litters he or she was raising when the puppy in which you are interested was growing up. A breeder who produces more than five litters a year—or who was raising three or four other litters while your puppy's litter was maturing—may not have had time to socialize every puppy in those litters properly. A breeder who raises one or, at most, two litters at a time has more opportunity to give each of those puppies the individual attention he or she deserves. In general, the fewer puppies a breeder produces, the more user-friendly those puppies will be.

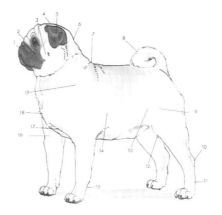

Buying a Show Dog

Persons interested in showing and eventually breeding their own pugs should start with the best-quality female they can find, preferably one with a champion-laden pedigree from a well-established kennel with an impressive show record. Novices also should remember that registration papers merely indicate that a dog is eligible to be registered, not that he is good enough to be shown. Any AKC-registered dog can be entered in a show, but there is a qualitative difference between a dog that can be shown and a show dog. The former is costume jewelry, the latter is a genuine pearl—often of great price.

Novices are at an even greater disadvantage evaluating a dog's show potential than they are when gauging his personality and general state of health. A runny eye is a runny eye to most observers, but eyes of the proper size, shape, and setting are more difficult for newcomers to identify. That is why a journey of a thousand dollars or more must begin with a few simple steps: Visit shows, talk to pug breeders, watch pug classes being judged, and learn what winning pugs look like. If possible, visit several pug breeders who are willing to spend an afternoon or evening "showing" their dogs at home.

The anatomy of a pug:
1. *muzzle*
2. *stop*
3. *cheek*
4. *skull*
5. *ear*
6. *crest*
7. *withers*
8. *tail*
9. *hindquarters*
10. *hock*
11. *metatarsus*
12. *stifle*
13. *loin*
14. *ribcage*
15. *pastern*
16. *forequarters*
17. *chest*
18. *brisket*
19. *shoulder*

Most important, study the pug breed standard. Take a copy of the standard and, if the breeder does not object, another breeder with you when you go to look at puppies. Ask the seller to point out where a puppy or a dog meets the standard and where he does not. And bear in mind that being pick of the litter is no guarantee that a puppy will be a judge's pick in the show ring.

Because breeders with the best available puppies will not always live within driving distance, you may have nothing more on which to base an informed decision than a few pictures and the breeder's evaluation. If the pictures are unclear, ask to see more. If you have any reason to doubt the breeder's word, find another breeder. In any case, ask the breeder to say, preferably in writing, where a puppy measures up to the standard and where he falls short.

Breeders usually will not guarantee a puppy's performance in the show ring. But a breeder should be willing to say if a puppy is champion material and to guesstimate the number of shows—10 to 15, 15 to 20, 20 or more—the puppy will need to earn his championship once he matures.

Anyone buying a show dog is also buying the constellation of genes that dog has inherited from his ancestors. The names and titles of the first four or five generations of ancestors are recorded on a dog's pedigree. The buyer should review a pedigree carefully to see how many members of a puppy's family are champions. The more champions present in a puppy's pedigree the better his ancestors have done in competition, and the better his chances, on paper at least, of carrying on the family tradition.

The buyer should not, however, be overly impressed with great-great- or great-great-great-grandparents. The important generations are the first two. A puppy inherits 50 percent of his genetic makeup from each of his par-

Hearing, seeing, and speaking no evil, three young couch-potatoes-in-training.

Pugs are a visual and tactile delight, as much fun to look at as to hold.

According to the AKC breed standard, a pug should have a "large, massive, round" head.

ents, 25 percent from any grandparent, and 12.5 percent from any great-grandparent. Each dog in the fourth generation contributes 6.25 percent to a puppy's genetic makeup. Obviously, dogs that far removed from the present are not going to make much of a splash in a puppy's gene pool.

Although some puppies never look anything but promising from an early age, the average youngster goes through several stages while he is growing up. The swan today can be an ugly duckling tomorrow. Will he be a swan again in due course? Perhaps. But how is the novice to know? That is why buyers should wait until a potential show-quality puppy has gone through the duckling phase before they sign any checks. Because different bloodlines go through the duckling phase at different ages, a buyer should ask the breeder when his or her puppies go off, and the buyer should wait until a potential show puppy has stopped quacking before making a final decision.

Contracts and Papers

Breeders should provide a sales contract when selling a puppy. Most contracts specify the price of the puppy; the amount of the deposit required to hold the puppy, if any; when the balance of the payment is due, and so on. Contracts also may specify that if at any time the buyer no longer can keep the puppy—or no longer wishes to keep it—the breeder must be given an opportunity to buy the puppy back at the going rate for puppies or dogs at that time. (A contract specifying that the breeder be allowed to buy the puppy back at the original price would most likely not hold up if challenged.) Finally, a contract should specify that the new owner has a definite period of time, usually three to five working days after receiving a puppy, in which to take him to a veterinarian for an examination. If the vet discovers any preexisting conditions, such as luxating patella or a heart murmur, the buyer should have the right to return the puppy at the seller's expense and to have the purchase price refunded.

When buyers give a breeder a deposit on a puppy, they should write "deposit for thus-and-such puppy" on the memo line of the check. They should make a similar notation when writing a check for the balance of the payment. Buyers should be given receipts for all payments, and they should find out in advance—and in writing if they wish—whether a deposit is refundable should they decide not to take the puppy. Buyers also should remember that once a breeder has accepted money or some other consideration in return for reserving a puppy, they have entered into an option contract; the breeder cannot legally revoke or renegotiate the offer—as some breeders may try to do—if the puppy turns out to be much better than the breeder had anticipated.

Buyers are advised to read a contract meticulously before signing it because contracts are legally binding once they have been signed by both parties. If a contract contains any stipulations that buyers do not understand or do not wish to agree to—like a stipulation saying that the dog must be shown to championship—they should discuss these issues with the breeder before signing.

In addition to the pedigree, new owners usually receive "papers" when they buy a pedigreed dog. These papers generally consist of a registration slip that the new owners fill out and send—along with the appropriate fee—to the administrative office of the American Kennel Club. AKC then returns a certificate of ownership to the new owners.

Persons buying a dog or puppy that already has been registered by his breeder will receive an owner's certificate. There is a transfer-of-ownership section on the back of that certificate that must be signed by the breeder and the new owner. Once the required signatures are present, the new owner mails the certificate, with the appropriate transfer fee, to AKC, which sends back a new, amended certificate of ownership to the new owner(s).

Health Certificates

Health certificates and vaccination and deworming records are the most important documents that accompany a puppy to his new home. Do not accept a puppy without these papers. Some breeders, especially those who produce a large volume of puppies, try to save money by giving vaccinations themselves. There is nothing illegal about this practice, yet there is more to immunizing a puppy than drawing vaccine into a syringe and pushing the plunger. Few, if any, breeders are capable of examining puppies as thoroughly as a veterinarian can before administering vaccinations. This examination is important because vaccine given to a sick puppy will do more harm than good. Thus, a puppy should be seen by a veterinarian at least once before he is sold, preferably before his first vaccination.

Helpful hint: Be sure that your puppy is accompanied by a health certificate issued by a veterinarian within ten days of the time you receive the puppy.

Life with a Pug

Next to acquiring a pug—and telling all your friends about this wonderful new dog you are getting—shopping for pug supplies is one of the great joys of being a pug owner. Limited only by your imagination and your credit-card balance, you set off for the pet-supply shop or the dog show determined to surround your pug with the trappings of the good life. Or, if you prefer to let your fingers do the shopping, you settle down with a beverage and a catalog from one of the pet-supply houses and phone in your order, scarcely taking your hand off the television's remote control while you do so. (See "Useful Addresses and Literature," page 92.)

A Shopping List for New Owners

No matter what your preferred mode of shopping, the following items should be on your shopping list:

Food and water bowls: These should be made of metal or ceramic. Reusable plastic can retain odors even if it is washed carefully. Disposable plastic is a burden on the environment. If you choose a ceramic bowl, make sure it does not contain lead, which can be poisonous to dogs.

Helpful hint: Whatever their construction, all food and water bowls should be solid and heavy enough not to tip over easily; ideally, they should have rubber guards on the bottom to prevent sliding. Also, food and water bowls should be sturdy enough not to break, crack, or chip if a dog knocks them over.

Place mats: Whether decorator vinyl or plain, utilitarian rubber, place mats will protect the carpet or floor under food and water bowls. This is no small consideration if your pug is the type who eats as though she were bobbing for apples.

Collar or harness: Collars are available in nylon or leather. A leather collar is fine for most adult pugs. Sturdy nylon-mesh collars, which are less expensive, are a better choice for puppies, who will need several collars while they are growing up. Because pugs are susceptible to respiratory difficulties if they become overheated, their collars must never be tight. You can check the fit of a collar by inserting two fingers between the collar and your pug's neck. If your fingers fit easily but snugly, the collar is properly adjusted. If you have to wedge your fingers in to make them fit, get your pug a larger collar or let this one out a notch or two. (Never put a choke

These are a few of pugs' favorite things. They should be made of metal or ceramic, not plastic. If you choose ceramic, make sure it does not contain lead, which can be poisonous to dogs.

chain—which is sometimes fatuously known as a check chain—on a pug.)

Some pug owners prefer to use a harness rather than a collar for walking their pugs because a harness does not put any pressure on a dog's windpipe. Lead-training is easier with a collar, however, so a harness usually is reserved for pugs that are lead-trained already. Whether she is wearing a collar or a harness, your pug should wear her license and identification tag whenever she leaves the house.

Lead: May be made of leather, cotton, or nylon. Some nylon leads are retractable. This feature permits you to keep your pug close by when necessary or to allow her to range more freely in open spaces.

Crate: The new pug owner's best friend, next to the new pug, of course, is the crate. Crates provide a feeling of security for pugs and their owners. Until your pug is house-trained, any time she cannot be with you, she should be in her crate.

The crate you buy should be large enough to accommodate your pug when she is grown, but small enough so that she will feel cozy in it when

When gathering supplies for your new pug, you should proceed as though you had just won a contest whose first prize is a shopping spree.

she is a puppy. A crate that measures 24 inches (61 cm) long, 21 inches (53 cm) high, and 19 inches (48 cm) wide meets those requirements. The bottom of the crate should be covered entirely with a soft mat equipped with a washable cover.

Food: For most pugs if the subject is food, the answer is yes. The pug's voracious appetite is legendary. One afternoon when I was in the puppy nursery about to take a three-day-old puppy's temperature, the phone in my office rang. When I returned to the nursery, which also doubles as our bedroom, there was our neutered fawn boy, Percy, with his head under the bed and his butt in the air. I assumed the same position to see what he was about.

He was about an inch and a half into the Vaseline jar I must have knocked to the floor when I went to answer the phone. He looked as if he had greased his face in preparation for a long-distance swim.

About 10:30 that night Percy leapt from the bed and quit the room at an agitated pace. We ushered him outside promptly. He looked much relieved after a few minutes, but one spot on our lawn suffered such an environmental insult that we feared nothing would ever grow on that spot again.

The chapter "The Well-fed Pug" (page 37) contains a brief treatise on canine nutrition. Armed with that knowledge and the cautionary tale of Percy and the Vaseline, the pug owner should be prepared for the life-long exercise in discipline that will be needed to prevent his or her pug from becoming overweight.

Grooming Tools: Regular grooming should be a part of every pug's routine. Pet-supply shops, mail-order houses, many veterinary offices, and vendors at dog shows carry the brushes, combs, shampoos, nail clippers, powders, ointments, sprays, and supplementary accouterments necessary for keeping your pug well groomed. The chapter "Routine Care and Grooming" (page 32) carries the instructions necessary to use these implements to best advantage.

Dog Beds: Pugs are great resters—so great, in fact, that a pug at full rest assumes the density of a black hole in space. The well-appointed house, therefore, contains a number of beds in which a pug can display her talents for resting. These beds should be deployed in rooms in which you spend a lot of time. This arrangement will allow your pug to combine two of its favorite activities: sleeping and being near you.

Dog beds are available in many sizes, colors, materials, and designs. But square-cut or pear-shaped, round or oval, bean bag, thinsulate, or medical-grade polyfoam, the most important characteristic of a dog bed is a removable, washable cover.

Toys: A brilliant array of dog toys, all of them contrived to provide hours of chewing pleasure, is available for your pug. Yet fun is not the sole criterion used in selecting toys for a dog. Toys must be safe as well. Balls with bells inside, for example, should be sturdy enough so that a dog cannot get the bell out and swallow it.

Helpful hint: Before buying a toy for your pug, try to imagine how the toy could cause harm. If there is any chance that it could, do not buy it.

Baby Gate: A sturdy, hinged, swing-open baby gate is essential for those rare times when you want to confine your grown, house-trained pug to a room in which you are not present. Puppies, as we have mentioned, are best left in their crates when you cannot be with them.

These pugs seem to be engaging in a game of Whisper Down the Lane.

Pug-proofing Your House

Pugs are built for comfort, not speed. Although they should be able to jump onto a sofa or a bed easily enough, they are not great leapers, and they are not so tall that they can stand on their hind legs and seize food off the kitchen table. Thus, pug-proofing your house consists mainly of keeping objects that you do not want chewed at an altitude where your pug cannot reach them.

In addition, if there are any rooms you do not want your pug to investigate, keep the doors to those rooms closed. If there are fragile objects in the rooms your pug is allowed to visit, put them out of reach. Make sure all sliding glass doors are closed securely and are marked in some fashion so that your pug does not go charging into them. Make sure all electrical cords are intact. If your dog or puppy begins chewing on electrical cords, wrap them in heavy tape or cover them with plastic tubes, which you can buy in an auto-supply shop. If necessary, until you are certain your pug has not developed a taste for electrical cords, unplug all appliances that are not in use. To keep your pug from getting a charge out of electrical sockets, cover them with plastic, plug-in socket guards, which you can buy at the hardware store.

Keep all kitchen and bathroom cleansers, chemicals, cleaners, and toilet articles in cabinets that can be closed or locked securely. Keep the lids on all trash receptacles tightly closed. Consider replacing trash containers whose swing-open lids could be dislodged if your pug overturns the containers. Put sewing supplies and yarn away when you are finished using them. Do not leave rubber bands, cigarettes, plastic bags, or pieces of string or yarn lying around.

Helpful hint: Learn to think like a pug. Look for any potential accident—tinsel on a Christmas tree or a dangling tablecloth—waiting for a pug to make it happen.

Welcoming the Newcomer

You have bought every item on your shopping list and a few extra items as well. You have set up the crate and dog bed(s). You have made a final safety check of the house. It is time to bring your new pug home.

Until your pug learns what is chewable and what is not, all electrical cords should be wrapped in heavy tape or covered with plastic tubes, which can be bought in an auto-supply shop.

If you work during the week, schedule homecoming for the start of a weekend or vacation. Remember that even though you have planned carefully for this day, it will come as a surprise to your dog—and as a major surprise to a puppy, who will be leaving her mother, playmates, people, and the only home she has ever known. Most puppies adjust swimmingly. They enter their new homes with wiggly excitement and great curiosity.

Other puppies (and older dogs) may not be so self-assured. Do not be surprised or insulted if your newcomer looks apprehensive. Keep the welcoming party to a minimum and continue stroking and speaking to your new pug gently. Once she has taken the measure of your household she will become more at ease, but that process should be taken one room and one or two family members at a time.

Helpful hint: Your pug will feel more comfortable in her new home if she has something from her former home on hand: a favorite toy, a blanket or bed, or a favorite food. These items give off familiar, comforting smells that are reassuring in a strange, new world.

Crate Training

The greatest security blanket you can give your new pug is a crate, and you should introduce her to her crate during her first hours in the house. After you have socialized with her for a while and have given her a chance to eliminate outdoors, place her in her crate with an interesting toy or treat. Leave the door open and stay in the room. (To establish their pugs' attachment to the crate, some owners feed their pugs their first meal in it.)

After your pug is used to sitting in her crate with the door open, latch the door the next time you put her in the crate. Stay in the room for a minute or two, tidying up or going about any sort of normal activity. Then let her out of the crate and tell her what a good dog she is.

Once your pug is used to the idea of staying in her crate with the door closed, leave her alone in her crate for a minute or two. Then return to the room and let her out of the crate, telling her what a good dog she is. (Your pug will learn to be relaxed about your comings and goings if you treat them matter-of-factly yourself, starting with the crate-training process.)

As you teach your pug to stay in her crate for progressively longer periods, you are preparing her to use it as her bed and safe haven, her own private wolf den. A dog will not soil her bed unless she is nervous or in dire need of eliminating. Thus, creating positive associations toward the crate will enable you to use it as an aid to house-training and as a secure place for your pug when you cannot supervise her.

Helpful hint: For the first few days after you bring your new pug home, however, you should keep her near you, even if this means placing the crate in one part of the house during the day and moving it to your bedroom at night. This will do much to ease your pug's adjustment to her new home.

House-training Without Tears

House-training a dog is simple. It consists of knowing that your dog has to relieve herself before she knows it. Fortunately, this is almost as easy as it sounds. If you understand a puppy's behavior patterns, she can be house-trained with minimal difficulty.

The younger the pug you acquire, the less likely she is to be house-trained, but no matter how young she is, she ought to have been paper-trained by her breeder. Paper-training begins when a puppy is about three weeks old, the age at which puppies

A pug's crate is his home within a home, a sanctuary to which he can repair when he is tired or when he wants to stop and think or when he merely wants to stop.

start to eliminate spontaneously. At this point, a breeder puts newspaper at one end of the cozy, blanketed nest the puppies share with their mothers. Young as they are, most of the time the puppies will take themselves to the newspaper when they have to eliminate. This is how puppies, who are born with an instinct to eliminate away from their nest, get the idea that newspaper is an appropriate surface for elimination.

This idea is reinforced when puppies are old enough to start romping around out of the nest—four to six weeks of age—but not old enough to go outside yet because they have not been vaccinated. By spreading news-papers over a large area of the puppy nursery during playtime, the puppies' breeder encourages them to continue using the paper for conducting person-al business.

If your pug is not house-trained when you get her, you will have to take her out of doors several times a day to the spot where you want her to eliminate. The first trip out should occur immediately after the puppy

last thing before going to bed for the night and whenever she begins sniffing the floor and pacing about in a preoccupied manner. All in all, this amounts to eight trips a day or so. What's more, very young puppies cannot defer elimination for more than roughly four hours. Therefore, you will need to take your pug out at least once during the night until she is three or four months old.

Do not expect your puppy to urinate and defecate every time she goes out. She ought to do one or the other on every trip, however, so do not take her back inside until you have given her ten minutes to perform. If she does draw a blank—or if your rapidly developing instinct tells you she owes you some urine or solid waste—take her back into the house, put her in her crate with a toy, and try her again in about half an hour to forty-five minutes.

As your puppy matures, she will need to go outside less frequently. After she is six months old, she will be eating twice a day instead of three

Somewhere between puppyhood and adulthood a pug's expression evolves from saucy (left) to sweet (right).

wakes up in the morning. Make sure she has urinated and defecated before you take her in for breakfast, and make sure you praise her as if her delivery were an envelope with Ed McMahon's name on the outside, declaring her a sweepstakes winner.

In addition to her morning constitutional, your pug will need to go outside about ten to fifteen minutes after each meal, immediately after waking up or engaging in spirited play, and any time she has been awake for two hours since the last time she was outside. She also ought to be taken outside the

Neither rain, nor sleet, nor the desire to roll over and go back to sleep can stay the dedicated pug owner from her puppy's appointed rounds—unless, of course, she enjoys cleaning up messes from floors.

times, making one less trip necessary, and she probably will not have to go out right after breakfast if she has gone out just before eating. Normally, our adult pugs go out upon rising at 4:30 or 5:00 A.M., about 9:30 in the morning, 1:00 or 1:30 in the afternoon, and following dinner, which is served between 4:00 and 5:00. If they are awake for several hours before retiring, we take them out one last time.

Although our dogs are used to going out at fairly short intervals, they are capable of waiting for longer periods if necessary. In fact, we have left them alone at home on a few rare occasions for as long as ten hours without mishap.

No matter how frequently you whisk your new (or old) pug out of doors, accidents will happen. This morning, for example, I did not notice that one of our pugs had not defecated during her 4:30 walk. It was snowing heavily, and she was in a hurry to get back into the house for breakfast. For my part, I was fantasizing about a cup of coffee. As a result, she soiled the kitchen floor at about 8:00 A.M. I am not a great one for blaming society for an individual's crimes, but had I been paying more attention to the dog, I would have kept her outside longer, or I would have taken her outside again after breakfast.

When a pug has an accident, I do not recommend scolding her or striking her or pushing her trusting, adorable face into her waste or putting her in her crate for punishment. After all, the damage has been done already. These ill-conceived reactions do nothing to further house-training. Scolding or striking your dog only teaches her that you are an unreliable and frightening brute. Stuffing her into her crate will make her associate the crate with negative feelings. These outcomes, as social scientists would say, are counterproductive. The secret of house-training—indeed, of all dog training—is to elicit the desired behavior from your dog, not to beat it into her.

Next to an observant owner, the puppy's crate is the most valuable aid in house-training. Because you have helped your puppy to learn that her crate is an inviting place, she will enter it willingly and use it as her bed during those times of the day when you cannot be with her. After she has been in her crate for any length of time, you should take her outside in case she has to eliminate.

Helpful hint: A puppy's physiological limit for controlling urination and defecation suggests that you should not acquire a pug puppy that is younger than four months old if no one will be home during the day. Also, keep in mind that an empty house is a lonely place for a pug puppy, a dog meant to spend her days as part of a family. For this reason, any pug living in a household where no humans are home in the day should always be one of at least two family dogs.

Playtime for pug puppies begins shortly after they awake; it ends seconds before they fall asleep.

HOW-TO:
Collar, Harness, and Lead

Introducing the Collar or Harness

The collar: Although pug puppies can adjust to a collar when they are seven or eight weeks old, there is no need to introduce the collar that soon. When your puppy is between ten and twelve weeks old, put a collar around her neck just before you feed her. Remove the collar after she has eaten but before you take her outside for her postmeal walk. After a few days, put the collar on her at other times during the day. Leave the collar on for a little longer each time. In about a week, add her identification tag and license tag to the collar. Our pugs do not wear collars in the house or when they are in

All tacked up and ready to go. When your pug must be under your control, your pug must be in a harness or collar.

the yard barking insults at the Doberman next door, but a pug should wear a collar whenever she leaves her property.

The harness: Introducing a harness to your pug is scarcely more complicated than introducing a collar. After spending a few minutes playing with and petting your pug, set the harness on her back. At this point, pug owners are of two minds regarding procedure. One mind says to attach the harness right away; the other mind says to let it lie on your pug's back a few seconds a day for several days before attaching it fully. The method you choose will depend on your pug's reaction to the harness. If she recoils in disap-

proval, pet her a few seconds, remove the harness tenderly, and try again tomorrow. If she does not seem to mind the harness, you might as well hook it up and be done with it. Be sure to give her a treat once the harness is in place. Do not give her a treat if she recoils from the harness. Reassurance is enough in that case.

After your pug consents to wearing the harness—which consent may be preceded by a period of rolling, scratching at the harness, and complaining—leave the harness on for five or ten minutes a day for several days. Then leave it on for 10 or 15 minutes a day and, finally, for 15 to 20 minutes a day after that.

28

Lead-training

Step 1: The lead should be added to the collar or harness in much the same way the collar and harness were added to your pug—gradually. The first time you put the lead on your pug, allow her to drag it around a few minutes and give her one or two treats during that interlude, then remove the lead. Repeat this routine for two or three days.

Step 2: Once your pug is comfortable with the lead, pick up one end and hold it. Do not try to lead her anywhere, simply hold the lead while she moves about, following her wherever she goes. Remove the lead after three or four minutes.

Step 3: Now you are ready to have your pug follow where you lead. To accomplish this, she ought to be on your left side, your left arm should be held naturally by your side, and the lead should be in your left hand. Turn your body toward your dog, show her the treat you have in your right hand, and take a step or two forward. If she steps toward the food—which she most certainly should—move a few additional steps forward. If she steps forward again, give her the treat. If she is reluctant to move, do not drag her. Move the food a little closer. As soon as she moves toward it, say "good," give her the food, and praise her for moving. If she refuses to move, pick her up, carry her forward to the place from which you called her, praise her for being a wonderful dog, but do not give her the treat. Then end the lesson for the day.

Steps 4, 5, 6 . . .: Your pug should be willing to move a few steps the first day you have her on a lead. On subsequent days, increase the distance she must walk alongside you before she gets her treat.

Lead-training 101 should be conducted in your driveway or backyard. Do not try a public thoroughfare until your pug walks attentively at your side.

Like any new lesson you present to your pug, lead training should be taught with large patience in small steps. New experiences can be unsettling for any animal. The easier you make the lesson, therefore, the more likely your pug is to grasp it readily. Remember that pleasing you is one of the most pleasing activities for your pug. Do not let your training methods put roadblocks on her path to happiness.

Introducing Children

Children who are too young or immature to treat a pug properly can pose a threat to her sense of confidence and safety. Children must be mature enough to understand that dogs do not like to be disturbed when they are eating or sleeping, that there is a right way to hold a dog, and that dogs are not toys to be lugged around the house. This is why parents with toddlers should wait to buy a dog or a puppy until their children are roughly four years old.

Before agreeing to sell a puppy or a dog, breeders often want to meet the buyers' children. Conversely, buyers with children might do best to seek breeders whose puppies have been raised with youngsters underfoot.

Children do not always understand that what is fun for them may be painful for a dog. Explain that they must be careful to watch where they walk and run when the dog is around. Explain, too, that dogs often are frightened by loud, unfamiliar sounds. Ask the children to speak and play quietly until the dog gets used to them. Caution them not to pick the dog up until you feel she is comfortable enough in her new surroundings not to be traumatized by an impromptu ride. Teach children the proper way to hold a dog: one hand under the dog's rib cage just behind the front legs, the other hand under the dog's bottom, with the dog's face pointing away from theirs. Have them practice this while sitting down in case they drop the dog or it jumps from their arms.

Dogs can inspire a sense of responsibility in children, but children never should be forced to take care of animals. And even when a child is a cooperative caregiver, parents should keep an unobtrusive eye on the dog's feeding schedule, trips outdoors, and general condition. Parents should remember also that when they buy puppies for their youngsters, they buy the puppies for themselves. Inevitably, even the most dog-responsible youngsters grow up and leave home, and they do not always take their dogs with them, especially when they go off to college.

The puppy's mother supervises or, perhaps, waits her turn to be held by this young man who obviously knows how to hold a pug properly.

Introducing Other Pets

You also should be cautious when introducing a pug to other four-legged members of the family. The chances of hostilities breaking out vary inversely with the age and tenure of the dog or cat already in residence. If you have an eight-year-old pet that has always been an only child, you probably should not get a new dog or puppy. If your pet is four years old or younger, you should be able to introduce your new pug if you manage the introduction carefully—and if you keep in mind how you would feel if a stranger suddenly was brought to your house for an indefinite stay without your prior approval.

If you have other pets, do not include them in the welcoming party when you bring your new pug home. Your cat should be confined in a room, and your dog should be in her crate. After you have fraternized with your new pug for a few hours, allow her to meet your dog. If you have more than one dog, introductions should be made one at a time.

The best way to introduce an older dog to a new one is to put the new dog in her crate before letting the old dog into the room. If the older dog sniffs at the puppy in curiosity but shows no hostility, put a lead on the older dog and let the puppy out of her crate. The less tension there is between the two dogs, the less tension you need on the lead. If your older dog flattens her ears or crouches ominously, tug on the lead with enough authority to keep her from reaching the puppy, escort her from the room, and try the introduction again the following day. If the introduction goes well, give each dog a treat, the older dog first, of course, to reinforce their civil behavior.

Before letting your cat in to see the puppy, be sure the cat's claws are clipped. As you would when introducing a dog to a puppy, place the puppy in her crate first, then let the two animals sniff at one another and exchange small talk. If your cat is lead-trained, put a lead on her when you bring her in to meet the puppy. If not, stay close to her and the puppy. Chances are a puppy-cat introduction is not going to go as smoothly as a puppy-dog introduction, but this does not mean that your puppy and your cat will not be able to coexist peacefully.

Weather and living conditions permitting, a pug should spend an hour or so each day outdoors.

Routine Care and Grooming

Grooming is the art of removing dead hair from a dog so he does not have to remove it himself. Like virtue, grooming is its own reward. The more dead hair you collect from your pug, the less you have to collect from the furniture, the rugs, or your clothing.

Although a pug's coat looks deceptively short, pugs do shed; and their hair has a life of its own—a half life, actually—that has been reckoned at 4 million years. If ever there is a nuclear war, the cockroaches that inherit the earth afterward will be wearing tiny sweaters made of pug hair.

Ordinary dog hair, when shed, tends to lie where it falls. Not pug hair. Just as pugs weave their way inextricably into your life, pug hair ingratiates itself into any fabric upon which it lands, thumbing its pushed-in nose at attempts to remove it with mere vacuum cleaners.

Even the 95-horsepower vacuum tractors that one sees demonstrated on infomercials at 3:00 in the morning are unable to extract all the pug hair from your carpets and furniture.

The Pug's Grooming Schedule

Pugs should remain smart-looking on two or three brushings a week, and you should not have to coax them to stand still during this procedure. Being the sensual creatures that they are, pugs thrill to the feel of a brush. When we want to groom our pugs, all we have to do is get out the brush and sit on the floor. We are surrounded immediately by four snorting, har-rumphing customers, all declaring by their importunings that theirs is the next appointment. (Pugs are equally congenial about being bathed, a subject taken up later in this chapter.)

The Right Tools

Before you begin grooming your pug, lay out the tools required for the task. You will need all of the following tools some of the time and some of the following tools all of the time. Your selection will be driven by the nature of the grooming session: a routine lick-and-a-promise maintenance or a close-attention-to-details makeover:

- brush(es)
- flea comb
- cotton swabs
- cotton balls
- nail clippers
- toothbrush and toothpaste

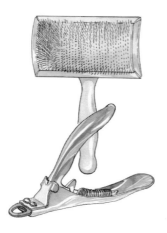

A slicker brush and nail clippers are two of the most important tools of the pug-grooming trade.

A smiling pug stands at attention while his smiling owner brushes him.

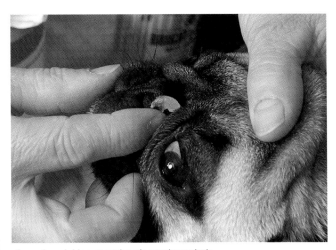

A pug's wrinkles must be cleaned regularly or they can become seedbeds of infection.

- lukewarm water
- Vaseline
- mineral oil
- paper cup or other receptacle for dead hair

A pin brush with stainless steel bristles is the best brush for a pug. If you want to be especially vigilant about removing dead hair, use a slicker brush. (The only comb you need for a pug is a flea comb, and you will need that only during flea season.)

Grooming Technique

Though informal grooming parties on the floor are mutually enjoyable for you and your pug, he should be groomed on a table at least once a week. Be sure to put a rubber mat or a piece of carpet with nonslip backing on the table to give your pug secure footing.

A well-raised pug puppy should not be a stranger to a brush. If your new pug is not used to being groomed,

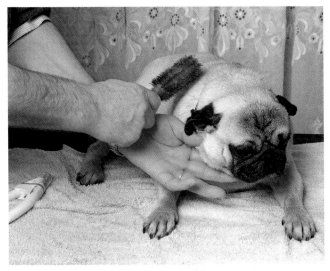

Pugs enjoy being groomed; some, like this one, even take it lying down.

training should begin as soon as he is settled in his new surroundings. Groom him four or five minutes every two or three days until he is used to being handled.

Always brush with the lie of the coat. Do not push down constantly on the brush. Move it across your dog's body smoothly with your wrist locked. In grooming young puppies and some older dogs you will need to wield the brush with one hand while you steady the dog with the other. For example, place your free hand on the puppy's chest while you brush his back and sides; or place your free hand, palm up, on his underbelly while you brush his hindquarters or neck.

A pug's legs are brushed or combed downward with short strokes. To groom a pug's tail, hold it by the tip, unfurl it gently, and brush or comb gingerly with the lie of the coat.

Brushing is required not only to keep your pug looking good but also to allow you to look for signs of trouble in his coat. While you are brushing, check for flea dirt, skin rashes, or bald spots. If you find flea dirt, a flea bath is in order. Skin rashes or bald spots merit a visit to the veterinarian, who can assess the problem and prescribe treatment.

A pug's nails are among the fastest-growing substances known to human-kind. They should be trimmed at least every other week.

Clipping Nails

A pug's nails are among the fastest-growing, hardest substances known to science. They must be clipped regularly to prevent any possibility of a pug scratching himself, his playmates, or his two-legged friends while playing. In addition, if your pug's nails are allowed to remain overlong, he will not stand as high on his toes as he should and may suffer a breakdown in the pasterns as a result.

Like all canines who have not become used to the idea of having their paws handled, a pug can turn rambunctious when anyone tries to clip his nails. One suspects, however, that this behavior reflects greater discredit on breeders who did not begin to clip their puppies' nails early enough than it does on their pugs. The person from whom you acquire your pug should have begun trimming his nails when he was two or three weeks old. If so, he ought to be acclimated to the process by the time he comes to live with you. If he is not, casually hold his paws or stroke them gently for a few seconds when you are petting him or watching television together. This contact will help to make him less sensitive.

Harvest time. Once or twice weekly the pug owner removes dead hair from his dog's coat.

Nail clipping, like death and taxes, is unavoidable. Treats and lavish praise will make the ritual more pleasant; so will having another member of the family hold your pug while you clip.

Be careful to clip the hooked part of the nail only. Avoid cutting into the quick, the vein inside the nail (see illustration). Have some styptic powder handy in case you do cut into the quick and it begins to bleed. Dip a Q-tip into the styptic powder and apply it to the bleeding nail. Apologize to your pug while the blood is coagulating and give him a treat afterward.

Ear Care

A pug's ears are not difficult to keep clean. A few cotton swabs or cotton balls and some mineral oil or hydrogen peroxide in a small container are the only materials you need. Dip the cotton swabs or cotton balls into the oil or peroxide (the choice is yours) and swab the visible parts of the ear carefully. Do not plunge the cotton swab or cotton ball down into the ear canal any farther than the eye can see, or you might do some damage.

Helpful hint: If you wish to clean your pug's lower ear canal, buy a cleaning solution from your veterinarian and follow the instructions faithfully.

Wrinkle-free Wrinkles

A pug's facial wrinkles, which contribute to his singular appearance, also may contribute to his discomfort—and to a certain clam-bog odor about him—if they are not cleaned regularly. Wrinkles, like the space between the cushions and the back of the couch, form a repository for excess food, tears, or other discharges from the eyes. Wrinkles must, therefore, be kept clean.

Once a week—or sooner if your pug's face begins smelling boggy—hold his head gently in one hand and, with a Q-tip that has been dipped in warm water, clean any dirt or caked tears from his nose wrinkle. Be sure to wield the Q-tip delicately. Pugs are proud of their faces, and they generally are disinclined to having you mucking about in their nose wrinkles.

Clean the smaller wrinkles under his eyes in the same manner, and after you have cleaned your pug's wrinkles, spread a thin application of Vaseline in them with a Q-tip. If you notice bald spots or a rash in the wrinkles, take your pug to the vet to determine whether he (your pug) is growing a fungus.

Like the crevices between sofa cushions and the back of the sofa, a pug's wrinkles attract debris. A weekly cleaning with a Q-tip will help keep the wrinkles free of infection.

HOW-TO:
Bathing Your Pug

Some people bathe their pugs in the kitchen sink. We find it more comfortable to bathe ours, once they are full grown, in the bathtub. Whichever you prefer, a spray attachment is a helpful option.

Before placing your pug in the tub, lay out the implements you will need for the bathing ceremony. These include:

• brush(es)
• regular or flea shampoo
• two or three bath towels
• cotton balls
• Q-tips
• mineral oil in a squeeze bottle
• hair dryer (optional)

Clean your pug's ears if necessary (see page 35) before putting him into the tub, and put a small wad of cotton into each ear to prevent water from reaching the ear canal and possibly causing infection. Put a few drops of eye ointment into

each of his eyes to protect them from stray shampoo. (If your pug's face needs washing, attend to that, too, before you bathe him.)

Put a rubber mat or a bath towel in the bottom of the tub to provide secure footing for the dog. Turn on the water and adjust the temperature, testing it with your wrist. If the water feels uncomfortably warm to you, chances are it will to your pug. Adjust accordingly until the water is comfortably lukewarm. Make sure, too, that the house temperature is at least 72°F (22°C).

If you are giving your pug a flea bath, wet his neck thoroughly as soon as you put him in the tub and then apply flea shampoo to his neck to prevent fleas on his body from hiding out on his face. Then wet down the rest of the pug thoroughly. Next, apply the shampoo, lathering the coat generously and leaving the shampoo in the coat for whatever length of time the manufacturer recommends

before rinsing. Never lather past your pug's neck or you risk getting shampoo into his eyes. If you use a regular shampoo, rinse your pug immediately after lathering.

After your pug has been lathered and rinsed—you are finished rinsing when the water coming off him is as clean as the water going onto him— remove him from the sink and wrap him in a towel. Use another towel to dry him more thoroughly. Because baths are stimulating for our pugs, we take them outside for a quick run after toweling them dry.

The Well-fed Pug

You need not take a home-study course in animal nutrition to feed your pug a balanced, nourishing diet. Indeed, you do not have to know a dispensable amino acid from an indispensable one—or the number of amino acids a dog requires—to be a good provider. All you need are a few fundamental coping strategies—which, of course, you will acquire by reading this chapter. Before we provide those strategies, however, we will present a brief discussion of the substances vital to a dog's well-being.

Proteins, Fats, and Carbohydrates

Protein, which comprises more than 50 percent of an animal's dry weight, helps to build and maintain cells, to provide energy, and to inspire muscle contractions. Digestive enzymes, insulin, the antibodies manufactured by the immune system, and most hormones are made of protein.

Dogs do not live by protein alone, despite its many functions in their lives. Dietary fat is another nutrient essential to a dog's survival. Fat is a concentrated energy source, a carrier for fat-soluble vitamins, and the wellspring of essential fatty acids needed to regulate a dog's metabolism.

According to the National Research Council (NRC), "All animals have a metabolic requirement for glucose [simple sugar] to supply energy for organs, including the central nervous system." Although carbohydrates are an excellent source of sugar, the NRC notes that as long as a diet contains "sufficient glucose precursors (amino acids and glycerol), the glucogenic capacity of the liver and kidneys is usually sufficient to meet the metabolic needs of growing animals for glucose without the inclusion of carbohydrates in the diet." Nevertheless, the NRC concludes, "Carbohydrates provide an economical source of energy in the diet of adult dogs." What's more, pregnant females need some carbohydrates in their diets for optimal reproductive performance.

Vitamins and Minerals

Dogs cannot reap the harvest from their food without the aid of vitamins, which combine with protein to create enzymes that produce hundreds of important chemical reactions. Vitamins also assist in forming hormones, blood cells, nervous-system chemicals, and genetic material.

Question: Do pugs eat to live, or do they live to eat? Answer: Both.

Although dogs mostly are affected by the lack of vitamins, an excess of vitamins, especially A and D, also can be harmful. Vitamin A toxicity, the consequence of a liver-rich diet, causes skeletal lesions. Vitamin D toxicity, the upshot of unwarranted supplementation, results in calcification of the aorta, the carotid arteries, and the stomach wall.

If a commercial dog food is labeled nutritionally complete and balanced (see "How to Decipher a Dog Food Label," page 40), do not add vitamins or supplements to it. Additional vitamins may upset the balance of vitamins already in the food and may cause vitamin toxicity. The only dogs needing vitamin supplements are those not eating properly because of illness or those losing increased amounts of body fluids because of diarrhea or increased urination.

In addition to vitamins, dogs need the following 12 minerals: calcium, phosphorus, sodium, potassium, chloride, magnesium, iron, copper, zinc, manganese, iodine, and selenium. Minerals help to maintain tissue structure, fluid balance, and the body's acid-base (electrolyte) balance. Because

mineral requirements are interrelated, the same warning about vitamin supplements applies to mineral supplements: proceed with caution and only on your vet's recommendation.

Water

Water is the most important nutrient needed to sustain normal cell function. Therefore, dogs should have fresh water in a freshly cleaned bowl every day. Mammals can lose nearly all their reserves of glycogen and fat, half their protein stores, and 40 percent of their body weight and still survive. The adult dog, composed of 60 percent water, is in severe metabolic disarray if she loses 10 percent of her body water, and death results if water loss rises to 15 percent.

The Pug's Desirable Weight

According to the American Kennel Club breed standard, it is "desirable" that pugs should weigh between 14 and 18 pounds (6.3–8.2 kg). But this is not a reliable guide to any single pug's ideal weight. A large-boned male 13 inches at the withers would be dolefully underweight at 14 pounds. A fine-boned female 10 inches at the withers would be close to obese at 18 pounds. Indeed, it is difficult to venture what any pug should weigh without knowing something about its bone structure, muscle development, and height.

Instead of looking only at the scale to determine if your pug exceeds or falls short of her desirable weight, look closely at your pug as well. If you can see her ribs, she is too skinny. If you run your hand gently down her back from shoulders to tail and you feel the spinous processes that stick out along the spine—or if during the same inspection you can feel the transverse processes that protrude sideways from the spine—she is too thin.

If your pug has an hour-glass figure or if you cannot feel her ribs readily, she is too fat. Additional bouquets of

fat are likely to blossom on the brisket (the area below the chest and between the forelegs), the neck, the abdomen, and the point at which the tail meets the body. If any of these spots seems too well padded, perhaps your pug is too well fed. (If you cannot see her ribs but you can feel them without having to squeeze her sides, she is probably neither too fat nor too thin.)

The Burden of Excess Weight

Whether you acquire a ten-week-old flurry of feet and kisses or a mature adult, there is a direct and incontrovertible relationship between what you put into your pug's bowl and the quantity of muscle and fat she develops. There also is a relationship between your pug's weight and her state of health. Although excess weight is wrongly indicted for causing everything from heart problems to dislocated kneecaps, there is no denying that too much weight is often a contributing factor—and is almost always a complicating one—in many health-compromising conditions.

In addition to aggravating locomotor problems, excess weight will aggravate collapsing trachea, an inherited condition common in toy breeds, in which the rings of cartilage in the windpipe collapse. Excess weight also makes it more difficult for pugs to dissipate heat in sultry weather, a problem already common to all members of the breed, fat or thin. Moreover, dogs, like people, are subject to an increasing litany of troubles as they grow older; pugs that are overweight when the specter of old age comes calling are saddled with an unfair handicap in fighting disease and infirmity. It is difficult to specify the point at which a pug's health could be compromised by surplus weight, but most females in excess of 19 pounds and most males in excess of 21 are candidates for less food and more exercise.

How Much and How Often to Feed

The amount of food a dog requires is determined by her age, condition, metabolism, environment, biological status, activity level, and ability to convert food into energy and heat. Variations in the effect of these factors among pugs can make generalizations, not to mention feeding charts, something of a risk. For example, three of our four pugs—two girls that weigh 18.2 and 18.5 pounds (8.2 and 8.4 kg) respectively and a 20.1 pound (9.1 kg) neutered male—get along nicely on two-thirds of a cup of dry food and about three ounces (85.1 g) of canned food a day. Our other pug, an 18.4 pound (8.4 kg) sprite with a hummingbird metabolism, needs almost one cup of dry food and about four ounces (113.4 g) of canned food a day to maintain her weight. We arrived at these precise calculations only after noticing that the sprite was beginning to lose weight even though the amount of food in her bowl was the same as that in her sister's, mother's, and uncle's bowls.

If there is one generalization that can be made regarding weight, it is this: The amounts specified in feeding charts on dog-food packages and cans are far too generous for pugs. Like the manufacturers of soap powder and shampoo, the makers of dog food usually overestimate the amount of their product a person needs to use in order to produce the desired results. The generosity on the part of dog-food manufacturers is understandable. They would be embarrassed if dogs were to lose weight on the recommended amounts. Therefore, they recommend high.

One manufacturer of a superpremium dry food, for example, recommends feeding 1.8 to 2 cups a day to dogs in the same weight range as ours. We feed only two-thirds to one cup of this food plus three to four ounces (85.1–113.4 g) of canned food daily. Even if we were to substitute an amount of dry food equivalent to the canned food we feed each day—about 4.6 ounces (130 g) of dry food—we still would be feeding a little more than half the manufacturer's recommended amount. (Other manufacturers are equally generous in their feeding recommendations.)

During their first year, pugs' food requirements diminish somewhat. From the ages of three to six months, our dogs ate three times a day. They each consumed a cup of dry puppy food, marinated briefly in warm tap water, and six to nine ounces (170–255 g) of canned all-life-stages food daily. When they were six months old, we switched to two meals a day. Each of those comprised one-half cup of dry puppy food, marinated briefly in warm tap water, and two ounces (56.7 g) of canned food. When they were a year old, we switched them to one-third of a cup of water-marinated dry food designed to fit all life stages of a dog and about an ounce and a half (42.5 g) of canned food twice a day. Subsequently, as noted above, we had to increase one pug's rations.

The well-fed pug has a well-read owner, who looks for assurances that the staples of a pug's diet provide complete and balanced nutrition for that particular stage—or for all stages—of a pug's life.

Switching Diets

When you get your pug, find out what kind of food she is used to eating. If that diet, whether commercial or homemade, is both sound for the puppy and convenient for you to feed, continue feeding it.

Helpful hint: If you want to switch foods—which you probably will if you buy a puppy that has been raised on a homemade diet and you would prefer to leave the measuring and stirring to the pet-food companies—fold a suitable new food into the puppy's previous food in a ratio of one part new to three parts old. Every three or four days increase the new food while decreasing the old until the changeover is complete.

How to Decipher a Dog-food Label

Reading a dog-food label is like squinting at the last line of type on an eye-examination chart. You cannot be certain if you are seeing what you think you are seeing, and even when you are certain, you are reading letters, not words. Letters like *m-e-n-a-d-i-o-n-e s-o-d-i-u-m b-i-s-u-l-f-i-t-e.*

Fortunately, there are only a few words a person needs to recognize in order to decipher a dog-food label. Most of those words are contained in the nutritional claim made by the manufacturer.

Nutritional claims come in two varieties. In the first the manufacturer declares that Bowser Bits has been shown to provide complete and balanced nutrition in feeding trials conducted according to protocols established by the Association of America Feed Control Officials (AAFCO). In the second kind of nutritional claim the manufacturer attests that Bowser Bits have been formulated to meet the nutrient levels established in AAFCO's nutrient profiles.

In order to make the feeding-trials claim, a manufacturer must compare data obtained from an experimental and a control group of dogs, each of which must contain at least eight members. The dogs in the experimental group are fed only Bowser Bits for a specified period of time. The control group is fed a diet known to be complete and balanced. At the end of the test period, if the dogs that were fed Bowser Bits do not differ significantly along certain variables from the control group, the manufacturer is entitled to claim that Bowser Bites provides complete and balanced nutrition according to AAFCO's feed-trial protocols. The variables on which the experimental and control groups are compared include weight, skin and coat condition, red-blood-cell count, and other health measures.

In order to make the second kind of nutritional claim—that Bowser Bits was formulated to meet nutrient levels established in AAFCO nutrient profiles—a manufacturer must sign an affidavit stating that he or she (or they) formulated Bowser Bits from ingredients that will contain, after they have been processed, sufficient levels of all the nutrients AAFCO has determined a dog food should contain.

The difference between buying a dog food that has been tested in feed trials and one that has been formulated to meet AAFCO profiles is like the difference between buying a preferred stock and a futures option: The consumer can be more confident that the preferred stock (the feed-tested dog food) is going to perform the way it is supposed to perform because it has been fed to real dogs in real feeding trials.

The meets-the-nutrient-profiles statement, on the other hand, is somewhat misleading. It does not mean that AAFCO has analyzed the food in question and has certified that it meets AAFCO standards. Nor does the statement necessarily mean that

the manufacturer tested the food in the can to determine whether it met AAFCO profiles. This statement simply means the manufacturer formulated the food from ingredients that should have provided enough nutrients to meet the AAFCO profile. We say "should have" because cooking always destroys nutrients in dog food to some extent. Therefore, the nutrients that go into the kettle are always present in greater amounts than the nutrients that go into the can.

Individual state regulators are responsible for checking the validity of nutritional claims. If a food is found wanting, the manufacturer is obliged to reformulate that food in order to provide sufficient levels of the nutrients that were lacking.

Some nutritional claims are conspicuous by their absence. Snack foods and treats (see page 45) do not have to contain any statement of nutritional adequacy. What's more, foods intended for intermittent or supplemental use only must be labeled so and should be used only on an intermittent basis.

Thus far we have discussed only one part of the nutritional claim made on dog-food labels: the part that tells you the basis on which manufacturers

The pug's "symmetry and general appearance are decidedly square and cobby," says the AKC standard.

41

state their claims. There is, however, a second part to nutritional statements: the part that specifies the dogs for which the food is intended. Thus, a complete nutritional claim for a feed-tested food will say: "Animal feeding tests using AAFCO procedures substantiate that Bowser Bits provides complete and balanced nutrition for all life stages of the dog." A complete nutritional claim for a meets-the-profile food will say: "Bowser Bits is formulated to meet the nutrient levels established by AAFCO nutrient profiles for all stages of a dog's life." Both these statements assure consumers that they can feed an all-life-stages food to their dogs from puppyhood through seniorhood, including motherhood, without worrying.

Instead of being formulated for all stages of a dog's life, some foods are intended for the maintenance of adult dogs only, and other foods are intended to support growth and reproduction. The latter are formulated to meet the increased nutritional needs of pregnant females and puppies. These foods must contain more of certain nutrients—more protein, calcium, phosphorus, sodium, and chloride, for example—than do maintenance foods. (Foods providing complete and balanced nutrition for all life stages of a dog must also meet growth-and-reproduction standards.)

No manufacturer ever went broke overestimating the dog's fondness for chewing.

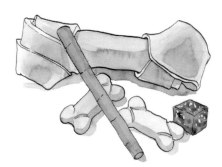

Some critics contend it is impossible for one food to be all things to all life stages of a dog. That argument need not concern nor confuse the pug owner. If you are feeding a pregnant female or a puppy, you should choose a growth-and-reproduction or an all-life-stages food. If you are feeding an adult pug, a maintenance food is sufficient and is, perhaps, less expensive than an all-life-stages food.

Several companies now produce senior-citizen foods for older dogs. These foods are based on two principles: older dogs need less of certain nutrients—proteins, phosphorus, and salt, for example—than do younger dogs; and older dogs are less able to tolerate nutrient excess than are younger dogs.

The jury and animal research are still out on the question of senior foods. It certainly cannot hurt to feed an older dog a senior food—which still must meet maintenance requirements in order to make the complete-and-balanced claim—but there is not at present enough evidence to show that senior foods help older dogs in any significant manner.

A Breakthrough in Labeling

One weighty piece of nutritional information that should soon be present on dog-food labels is the food's caloric content. Previously, the cost of monitoring caloric claims prohibited states from allowing manufacturers to state caloric content. But in 1992 AAFCO accepted a procedure designed by its feline-nutrition-expert (FNE) subcommittee that allows states to verify by laboratory analysis the caloric-content claims made by manufacturers for their products. In early August 1993 the CNE's recommendation was approved and was passed into regulation.

"Caloric-content information is probably more important than the current information on pet-food labels," says

David A. Dzanis, D.V.M., Ph.D., and chairman of the CNE subcommittee. "Knowing the caloric content will enable consumers to make informed comparisons between products because consumers will have a meaningful way of determining that it is possible to feed X amount of this product and get the same effect as feeding X amount of another product."

Dry, Semi-moist, or Canned?

Dog food can be divided into three genres: dry, semi-moist, and canned. Dry food is less expensive, easier to store, and more convenient to use than is canned food, and dry food helps to reduce dental plaque to some extent. Canned food is generally more palatable and, since it is three-quarters moisture, is a better source of water than are other foods. (Dry food contains roughly 10 percent water. Semi-moist contains 33 percent water.)

Dry food is the most popular among dog owners. Of the 3.9 billion pounds (1.8 billion kilos) of dog food purchased through supermarkets and other retail outlets in 1991, dry-food purchases accounted for 51 percent (1.98 billion pounds). Canned food was second in popularity, accounting for 29 percent of dog-food sales (1.13 billion pounds).

Generic, Private Label, Regular, or Superpremium?

Besides having three categories of dog food from which to choose, pug owners can select generic, private-label, regular, or superpremium brands.

Generic dog foods, which often do not carry a brand name, usually are produced and marketed locally or regionally, thereby reducing transportation costs and enabling merchants to sell generic foods at cheaper prices. But if generic foods are produced from cheaper materials, they may not provide the nutritional quality of private-label, regular, or superpremium foods. Before you buy a generic brand, look for the nutritional-claim statement on the label and, just to be safe, buy only those generics whose claims of nutritional adequacy are based on AAFCO feeding-trial procedures.

Private-label foods, which usually bear the house-brand name of a grocery-store chain, may be manufactured by the same companies that produce generic dog food or they may be manufactured by nationally known companies that also produce their own, more recognizable brands. Instead of the traditional "Manufactured by...." statement that appears on the labels of generic, regular, or superpremium foods, private-label brands will contain one of the following statements: "Distributed by...." or "Manufactured for...." The same advice offered regarding generic dog food applies to private-label brands, too. For greatest security, buy only feed-tested products.

Regular brands are foods with nationwide distribution and nationally recognizable names. There are usually no special nutritional claims made for regular dog foods, beyond, of course, the claims that they are good for your dog and that they meet AAFCO requirements.

Superpremium brands command top dollar and are made with top-of-the-line processing techniques that, manufacturers claim, reduce nutrient loss during heating. Moreover, say manufacturers, superpremium foods are made from higher-quality ingredients: chicken necks or backs instead of chicken by-products such as lung or bone. All this, manufacturers contend, results in foods with taste, smell, texture, and digestibility superior to other kinds of dog food.

Some authorities do not believe, however, that chicken necks are any more nutritious than chicken by-products or that a manufacturer's devotion to aesthetics results in more nutritional miles to the gobble. "Higher-quality ingredients and higher palatability do not make premium foods any better than regular foods," says Quinton R. Rogers, Ph.D., professor of physiological chemistry at the school of veterinary medicine, University of California. "Once you've met the nutritional requirements, you've met them." Thus, a superpremium food with twice as many vitamins as a regular food is not necessarily better, let alone twice as good as the regular food. The dog eating the superpremium food, Rogers explains, just loses the excess vitamins in her urine.

Devotees of superpremium foods also claim that their higher digestibility results in lower fecal volume and less fecal odor. The toxicity of fecal odor being in the nose of the beholder, it is impossible to investigate the second of those claims objectively. The lower-fecal-volume claim could be tested, but as one nutritionist has observed, there is little benefit (accrued or otherwise) in scooping up a 50-gram dog dropping vis-a-vis a 60-gram pile. (This difference did become significant, however, when the author and his wife were raising a litter of six pug puppies.)

Manufacturers also claim that superpremium food costs no more to feed than does regular food because dogs eat less of superpremium than they do of regular food. This claim can be tested easily. If you are feeding your dog one can of food a day that costs 48 cents and you are considering switching to a superpremium brand that costs 64 cents a can for the same amount of food, you should be able to feed your dog 48 cents worth of the superpremium food—or three-quarters of a can instead of the whole can you are presently feeding.

To test this theory, weigh your dog on the day you switch to the superpremium brand. Then weigh her again a month later. If she has gained more than two or three ounces, cut back on the superpremium food. If she has lost more than two or three ounces, you will have to increase the amount of superpremium food slightly. Obviously, if your pug has gained weight, the superpremium food costs less to feed than the regular food; but if she has lost weight, the superpremium food costs more.

Consumers also should be aware that superpremium dog foods do not have to meet higher standards than do regular foods. In fact, says Dzanis, "there is no official definition or clear-cut standard by which to judge superpremium food as far as the Food and Drug Administration and AAFCO are concerned. Their role is to insure that products are safe and wholesome. Beyond that, it's a consumer issue, like choosing between chuck steak or filet mignon."

Special Diets

Dogs suffering from various diseases often need special diets. For example, dogs with hypertension, heart disease, or edema should be on low-sodium diets. Dogs with kidney or liver conditions should be fed diets low in protein, phosphorus, and sodium. Dogs that are underweight or that suffer from pancreatic or liver disease should be fed highly digestible food. If any of these or other conditions are diagnosed by a veterinarian, he or she may recommend a special diet. Pug owners should follow the veterinarian's instructions faithfully, and, of course, they should never feed a special diet to a pug without first consulting with a vet.

Snacks and Treats

Although no one is a hero to his or her valet, pug owners become instant deities whenever they rattle a box of snacks. There is no more joyous and attentive audience than pugs contemplating a treat. Their nostrils flare, they dance imploringly on their hind feet, their bodies quiver from head to tail, their breath comes in fiery snorts, and their eyes threaten to pop out of their heads.

A considerable subset of the pet-food industry is built on this response. Pug owners who become too addicted to the positive reinforcement provided by a food-mongering pug are feeding their dogs as well as their egos, however. Snacks and treats are nutritionally deficient for full-time use, and your pug is going to want them full time if you offer them too frequently.

You can feed some foods to your pug all of the time and you can feed all foods to your pug some of the time, but nutritional wisdom is the better part of knowing which time is which. Again, let the label be your guide. If the label says, "Bowser Beef Wellington Bits are

Pugs are always ready to choose up sides and play.

intended for intermittent or supplemental use only," then use them intermittently. Do not allow snacks and treats to comprise more than 5 to 10 percent of your dog's diet.

Chew Toys

No entrepreneur ever went broke overestimating the dog's fondness for chewing. Upon meeting a strange object, a dog generally exercises one of two options: If it moves, the dog barks at it. If it stands still, the dog gnaws on it. That is why supermarkets, pet shops, and feed stores bristle with an al dente selection of chewables.

Chew toys are based on the principle that a dog's teeth are certified erogenous zones. If you want to send a dog into terminal euphoria, bring home a sweaty, smoked and processed pig's ear, set it on the floor, and announce, "Let the gnawing begin." Several hours later your dog will have achieved a state of bliss known only to Tibetan mystics.

Chewables, like any other source of pleasure, also can be a source of pain.

If pugs are fed too much people food, eventually they may not want their own. Then their owners will be doing the begging.

45

Chicken bones should be avoided entirely because they can splinter, get lodged in a dog's throat, or poke holes in his stomach or intestines. In fact, some observers warn that all bones, even marrowbones and knucklebones, can splinter. This is, perhaps, more likely to occur with larger breeds than it is with pugs. We have been giving our pugs marrowbones and knucklebones without harmful incident for some time. (Most pug owners who do give marrowbones or knucklebones roast them in a 175° oven for 20 minutes to kill any harmful bacteria.)

Processed cow hide, generally known as rawhide, is the astroturf of the bone world. Long aware of the dog's fondness for chewing, pet-supply manufacturers routinely paint, process, and press rawhide into "bones" for your dog's chewing enjoyment. Some rawhide bones are a bleached-looking white, others an off-cream, and still others, which have been basted, broiled, or roasted come in colors for which there are no words. In addition to being basted or roasted, some bones are chicken, beef, hickory, cheese, peanut butter, or (for those pugs expecting company) mint flavored. Because of its flexibility, rawhide also can be fashioned into surreal approximations of tacos, lollipops, cocktail franks, bagels, french fries, and giant pretzels to appeal to human tastes.

This pug is taking a breather in the middle of a serious discussion with a rawhide bagel.

A splintered chicken bone is not a pretty sight. Nor is a pug who comes to grief because her owner gave her a chicken bone to chew.

There is the possibility that a dog can come to grief by chewing off pieces of rawhide and swallowing them. Be sure to monitor your pug carefully the first few times you present her with a rawhide chew toy. If she shows an inclination to chew off pieces of the toy, give her something more substantial to chew on instead—such as a bone made of hard nylon.

Helpful hint: Given manufacturers' ingenuity, one suspects that soon it will be possible to give a dog a different chewable treat every day of the year without giving a treat of the same size, shape, color, and flavor more than once. But whether your pug prefers rawhide watermelon slices or marrow bones tartare, all chewables should be served inside the house. A pug gnawing happily on a chewy treat in the backyard soon will be attended by a retinue of ants, flies, bees (if they are in season), and other uninvited vermin. We learned this lesson when one of our pugs came in from the yard with one half of her lip swollen into what looked like a canine imitation of an Elvis snarl.

The Healthy Pug

Pug dogs reveal their state of health by the way they look and behave. Their eyes are bright and gleaming. Their noses are cool and slightly damp. Their gums are neither pale nor inflamed. Their ears are free of dirt and wax. Their bodies are fit and well muscled, a little padded, perhaps, but not paunchy and never seriously thin. Their coats are plush and immaculate without bald patches, scabs, or flea dirt. The area below their tails is unmarred by inflammation, dried waste, lumpy growths, or discoloration.

Although they spend prodigious amounts of time in sleep—a good 14 to 16 hours a day—pugs are otherwise active and alert. They display affection for their owners, a zest for adventure, a fearless approach to life, and a keen interest in mealtimes.

If Symptoms Persist

Frequently the first suggestion that a pug is unwell is a lack of interest in food. One missed meal or a faint, desultory pass at the plate is cause for some apprehension; the pug that misses two consecutive meals merits a call to the veterinarian, who probably will want to know if that pug's temperature is elevated or if he displays additional symptoms of potential illness such as vomiting or diarrhea.

Do not worry about making a pest of yourself by calling your veterinarian whenever your pug does not seem right. No caring vet will be annoyed by hearing from a caring owner, no matter how slight the symptom(s). And do not hesitate to seek another opinion if you have any reservations about the way your veterinarian is treating your pug.

When our pug Debbie was 15 months old, she woke up sneezing about 3:00 one Saturday morning. Because her nose was a little runny, too, we had her at the vet's by 9:30. Her lungs sounded normal, her temperature was not elevated, and she had eaten breakfast. Thus, the vet concluded that Debbie might be growing an upper respiratory infection. We left the office with some antibiotics and instructions to call back on Monday if Debbie was not well.

Over the weekend Debbie became more lethargic and less interested in eating. When the vet reexamined her on Monday, Debbie's lungs were taking on fluid, her temperature was elevated, and the diagnosis was pneumonia. We left the office with stronger antibiotics, a diuretic, and instructions to call again if Debbie was not well by Thursday.

I feared that Debbie was not going to be around by Thursday at the rate she was going. When she would not eat at all Monday night or Tuesday

A pug who is uninterested in eating is a pug who is probably not feeling well.

morning, I called another vet and was in his office with Debbie by 7:30 that night. After examining the dog, he informed my wife and me that Debbie would not be going home with us. He planned to quadruple her diuretic and put her on intravenous antibiotics and fluids. He also was going to do a cardiogram and consult by phone with specialists in New York.

We called the vet twice on Wednesday. The second time I called he said Debbie had begun to eat. I asked if we might visit her on Thursday. He said that was all right.

We arrived on Thursday with our other pug and half a pound of white-meat turkey from the delicatessen. When Debbie fell on the turkey and then tried to assume the dominance position by putting her front legs on our other pug's shoulders, we fairly broke into cheers.

Debbie was released the next day. She had to go back to the veterinarian's for x-rays twice during the following weeks to make sure the fluid had receded from her lungs. I am convinced the second vet saved her life. I hope you are convinced that one of your many functions as a pug owner is that of medical advocate.

This curious adolescent is all eyes, ears, and alertness.

A Brief Veterinary Checklist

Lack of interest in food is not the only, or always the first, sign of illness. You should call your veterinarian if the answer is yes to any of the following questions:
• Is your pug's breathing labored?
• Has he been coughing, gagging, or sneezing?
• Has he been favoring one leg when he walks?
• Is he drinking more water than usual?
• Is he dragging his hindquarters across the floor?
• Does he have a swelling or an abscess on his body?
• Is he scratching, licking, or chewing himself excessively?
• Is there an immoderate amount of flea dirt in his coat?
• Are his eyes runny, cloudy, or bloodshot?
• Have you noticed worms in his stools?
• Is there blood in his urine or stools?
• Has he been shaking his head frequently?
• Has he been lethargic for any length of time?
• Has he been digging at his ears?
• Are his gums inflamed?
• Is his nose runny?
• Is his breath foul?

Vaccinations

Until they are roughly six to eight weeks old, puppies are protected from certain diseases by antibodies in their mothers' milk, as long as their mothers have been immunized properly against those diseases and possess sufficient antibodies to confer immunity. Because this passive immunity interferes with puppies' ability to produce antibodies in response to vaccination, they are not vaccinated for the first time until they are at least six weeks old.

48

The vaccine given to puppies contains antigens that have been derived ultimately from viruses or bacteria obtained from live animals. Typically, a six-week-old puppy is vaccinated against distemper, hepatitis, parainfluenza, parvovirus, and leptospirosis. In areas where the bacterial disease leptospirosis is not a problem, veterinarians may vaccinate against coronaviruses instead. All of these diseases are debilitating and potentially fatal. Therefore, all puppies should be vaccinated according to schedule.

The antigens representing the above-mentioned diseases are usually administered in a single vaccine. When those antigens begin circulating in the puppy's bloodstream, they are detected and seized upon by specialized cells that are part of the body's immune system. After a series of complex evolutions, the puppy's immune system produces cells that are able to detect and destroy the diseases represented by the antigens in a vaccine. Thus, if a dog vaccinated against distemper was later exposed to the virus, distemper antibodies would recognize and exterminate any free-ranging distemper virus particles at large in the bloodstream. And if the distemper invaders managed to infect some of the dog's cells, those infected cells would be recognized, destroyed, and shown the door by other specialized cells in the immune system.

One vaccination, however, does not confer instant immunity on a puppy. Not for five to ten days will a puppy's immune system start to forge a response to the challenge posed by the antigens in a vaccine. That response is low grade and not entirely effective. What's more, one can never be certain how long a puppy's passive immunity will continue to compromise his ability to manufacture his own antibodies. For these reasons all veterinarians revaccinate a puppy in three to four weeks, and many veterinarians revaccinate again four weeks after the second vaccination. After that, dogs should receive booster shots once a year because antibodies decrease in number over time and the immune system needs to be stimulated to produce additional disease-fighting troops.

The initial rabies vaccination is administered to dogs when they are three months old. Most veterinarians boost that shot when a dog is a year old and then boost it every year or two thereafter.

Puppies should be vaccinated at six, ten, fourteen, and (some veterinarians say) eighteen weeks of age. They also should receive booster shots annually.

External Parasites

Parasites are living organisms that reside in or on other living organisms (called hosts), feeding on blood, lymph cells, or tissue. Internal parasites dwell inside their hosts. External parasites live on the surface of their hosts.

The external parasites to which a dog is the unwitting landlord include fleas, ticks, flies, lice, larvae, and mites. This motley collection of insects and arachnids, in addition to damaging skin tissue, may transmit harmful bacteria and menacing viruses to your pug. In significant quantities external parasites can sap your pug's energy, weaken his resistance to infection and disease, and bequeath to him a number of diseases and/or parasitic worms.

The presence of external parasites is usually revealed by flea dirt, skin lesions, pustules, hair loss, itching, redness, dandruff, scaling, scabs, growths of thickened skin, or an unpleasant odor. If your pug begins to scratch or bite at himself excessively or if you notice any of these symptoms while you are grooming him, call your veterinarian. She or he will prescribe a course of treatment. The earlier external parasites are detected, the easier they are to banish. This, among other reasons, is why you should groom your pug two or three times a week.

Humans, too, can be affected by some of the external parasites troubling their dogs. If flea infestation is severe enough, fleas may dine out on humans temporarily. Certain kinds of mites will migrate to humans, and so will ticks. Especially worrisome to humans are ticks that carry Rocky Mountain spotted fever and Lyme disease. The latter is the most common tick-borne disease in the United States.

Pugs afflicted with external parasites will have to be treated with parasiticidal dips, powders, ointments, and/or shampoos. Always follow your veterinarian's instructions when using these products.

Waging War on Fleas

Eternal vigilance is the price of a flealess pug. There are many shampoos, sprays, powders, mousses, bombs, roll-ons, flea collars, and dips designed to kill fleas. Before using any of them, consult your veterinarian and use them according to instructions.

Insecticidal flea collars do not light up the scoreboard with flea kills, and some dog owners are concerned about the harm done by pesticides in these collars. Before putting a flea collar on your dog, remove the collar from its sealed package and snap it taut a few times to shake off excess insecticide. Wash your hands immediately. Let the collar air out (away from pets and children) for 24 to 36 hours before putting it on your pug. Watch him closely for several days to be sure no sores appear. If they do, if the dog seems groggy, or if he develops nasal irritation or inflamed eyes, remove the collar at once. Collars that get wet must be removed and dried. Many collars are no good once they are wet, and should be discarded.

Additional weapons in the war against fleas include ultrasonic flea collars, food-grade diatomaceous earth (sold in hardware stores and garden-supply centers), and various vitamins and oils. Ultrasonic collars do not sound like much of a threat to fleas. A study conducted at the School of Veterinary Medicine, Purdue University, evaluated two brands of ultrasonic flea collars. Each was tested on a group of five cats for a seven-day period. During that period cats in a control group wore no collars. At the end of the study, cats that had worn ultrasonic flea collars were still wearing 98.6 percent of their fleas. Cats that had not worn collars retained 97.4 percent of their fleas.

Diatomaceous earth is sprinkled into rugs and upholstery on the theory that it causes fleas to dry up and die upon contact. Brewer's yeast is added to a dog's food and dusted into his coat and bedding. Garlic is added to food; vinegar to a dog's drinking water. Chelated zinc, lecithin, cod liver oil, cold-pressed, unsaturated vegetable oil, kelp, and vitamin C also are touted as flea remedies. Scientists and most veterinarians, however, are skeptical about the value of these remedies.

Internal Parasites

Protozoa and worms are the internal parasites to which a dog is host. Protozoa are usually one-celled organisms that may contain specialized structures for feeding and locomotion. One protozoan sometimes found in dogs is *Toxoplasma gondii*, which is carried in oocysts shed in cat feces. If you have a cat, do not allow your pug to go truffle hunting in the litter box. Fortunately, the threat of your pug's being infected by *T. gondii* from your cat is limited. Once a cat's immune system responds to *T. gondii*, the cat stops shedding oocysts. (Coccidia, another protozoan disease, is usually found in young dogs kept in crowded conditions.)

The presence of three kinds of worms that infest dogs—roundworms, hookworms, and whipworms—can be detected through stool-sample analysis. Tapeworms, however, are not amenable to this method of identification. They are best identified by lifting a dog's tail and looking at his anus. During this examination, you are looking for small, white tapeworm segments that look like grains of rice. These segments can also be seen on fresh stools.

The presence of heartworms can be detected by blood-sample analysis. If your pug is negative for heartworms, your veterinarian can prescribe preventive medication to keep him that way. If your pug tests positive for heartworms, he will require treatment that may include hospitalization and/or surgery.

Most worms, despite their repugnance, are not difficult to control. When you acquire a pug, ask the person from whom you get him when the pug was last dewormed and what deworming agent he was given. To be safe, take a stool sample and your new pug's previous deworming history to your veterinarian. She or he will recommend a safe, effective deworming agent and will set up a deworming schedule.

Keeping the Pearly Gates Pearly

Clean teeth, in addition to being things of beauty and a joy, one hopes, forever, may help to prevent certain diseases of the heart, liver, and kidneys that are thought to be caused by the spread of bacteria from a dog's mouth. Diligent pug owners, therefore, do not allow poor dental hygiene to put the bite on their dogs' health.

Dry dog foods, which ought to comprise the bulk of a pug's diet (see "The Well-fed Pug," p. 37), help to a certain extent to reduce plaque—the sticky combination of bacteria, food particles, and saliva that is constantly forming and hardening on a pug's teeth. Unfortunately, dry foods are not an unalloyed dental blessing. The carbohydrates in dry foods stick to the teeth and act as compost for the bacteria that is plaque's main ingredient. (Canned dog foods do nothing to remove plaque. What's more, the sugar they contain adds to its buildup.)

Pugs are willing to assist in their own dental care by chewing on rawhide bones, knucklebones, marrowbones, or bones made of hard nylon. Encourage this participation by allowing your pug to chew on some kind of bone or specially designed teeth-cleaning toy once or twice a week.

If plaque is not removed regularly from your pug's teeth—by you or by your pug—it hardens into calculus (tartar) and intrudes itself between the teeth and gums, creating a tiny sinkhole in which bacteria multiply. These bacteria invade the gingiva (gum), causing it to become inflamed and swell, and to bleed when probed. This condition, known as gingivitis, is reversible if treated early in its development. If not, it escalates into periodontitis: ulceration of the gums and erosion of the alveolar bone, which holds the teeth in place.

HOW-TO:
Flea-bomb Your House

Know the Enemy

Fleas are older than dirt and uglier than sin. These lean, mean, blood-sucking machines are armor-plated, bad to the bone (figuratively), and able to leap 150 times their own length, vertically or horizontally. And if you want to talk stamina, one rat flea was clocked jumping 30,000 times without stopping.

Preparing for liftoff, the flea crouches with malicious intent. Its leg and thorax muscles compress a tiny pad of superelastic protein called resilin. Then a complex mechanism triggers an explosive release of resilin energy, and *Shazaaam!* the flea shoots from cat to carpet or carpet to cat or one cat to another faster than you can say, "Die, you "&#%*@#%&*""—and 50 times faster than a space shuttle accelerates after liftoff.

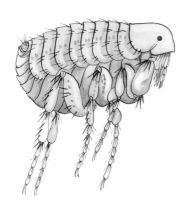

Fleas can survive months without eating, and they are able to remain frozen for a year, then revive and conquer. As same-day couriers for bubonic plague, they have taken out more people than war itself: 40 million from 541 to 741, another 25 million in Europe alone between 1347 and 1352, and 6 million in India during one decade in a plague that came out of China in 1855 and still lingers in parts of the world today.

Considering the flea's numbers and nastiness, it is obvious that if your pug and your house become infested with fleas despite your diligent efforts to the contrary, you will need to launch a major offensive to reclaim the lost territory. Simply giving your pug a flea bath will not do. If you are treating only the fleas on your pug, you are treating only 10 percent of the problem. The other 90 percent is merrily ensconced in your house, waiting for a chance to pounce.

Preparing for the Attack

When the morning of your major offensive dawns, leave your pug at the veterinarian's for a flea bath and dip, which you will, of course, have scheduled in advance. When you return home, vacuum the house obsessively. Vacuuming is important because carpets, furniture, baseboards, bedding, cracks in the floor, and your pug's favorite resting places are the staging areas where flea eggs, larvae, and pupae (the other 90 percent of your flea problem) develop. Flea eggs, four to eight hundredths

of an inch long, incubate for two to twelve days. Then they hatch into larvae—tiny, white, bristled worms that feed mainly on popcorn nuggets, shards of Dorito chips, and fecal casts from adult fleas. After growing—and molting twice—over a period of nine to two hundred days, larvae molt one more time, turning opaque, becoming quiescent, and spinning a loose, whitish-gray cocoon in which they remain for seven days to a year.

Put naphthalene crystals or crushed moth balls in the

vacuum cleaner bag or else it will become a traveling flea incubator. When the vacuum bag is full, seal it tightly and bury it in the nearest toxic waste dump. Failing that, put it in an outdoor trash can with a tight lid.

Bombs Away!

When you have finished vacuuming, flea dip all your pug's washable bedding. Without rinsing it, run the bedding through the washer's spin-dry cycle, then hang the bedding outdoors to dry. Next, close all the windows in the house and set off aerosol foggers in every room. The best bombs are the ones that contain IGRs (insect growth regulators), which prevent immature fleas from maturing. Then spray the grass and shrubbery around the house with an insecticide. (Some people spray their yards periodically throughout the flea season.) Then go out to eat.

Mopping-up Operations

When you return home, open the windows throughout the house and allow the rooms to air out. Do not bring your pug back home sooner than the instructions on the bomb labels recommend. If there is no recommendation of this sort on the label, consult your veterinarian. You may have to leave your pug at the vet's overnight and not bring him home until the next day.

Once your pug has been bathed and dipped and the house has been bombed, continue vacuuming and flea-combing daily. Fleas removed from your dog can be drowned in a dish containing a little flea dip, or they can be crushed gleefully by fingernail. If you see a lot of fleas during your daily combing, dip the dog again the next weekend. If you are not taking any fleas off your dog, it is probably safe to vacuum every other day. If the fleas return en masse, you will have to repeat the D-day flea offensive.

Periodontitis is not reversible, and if it is not controlled, the gums and alveolar bone eventually become so eroded that the teeth fall out.

To check for signs of gingivitis, gently but firmly hold your pug's head with one hand and lift his upper lip along one side of his mouth with the other hand. Look closely at his teeth and gums. Repeat this procedure on the opposite side and in the front of his mouth. Then inspect his bottom teeth in the same fashion. If there is a red line along his gums, make an appointment to have your veterinarian check your pug's teeth.

Other signs of oral disease include perpetual morning breath, avoidance of dry food, resistance to being stroked on the muzzle, brown or yellow crust on tooth surfaces, loss of appetite, and drooling. If your dog exhibits any of these symptoms, call your vet and describe the dog's behavior.

You can assist your pug in keeping his teeth clean by brushing them once or twice a week. Introduce this idea gradually by playing a game of "See the Doggie's Teeth" each day. Look at his teeth as you did during the gingivitis inspection, but in addition to just looking, rub a finger along his teeth, first in front of them and then behind them.

When your pug is used to this game, substitute a soft-bristle child's toothbrush or a finger brush made especially for dogs in place of your own finger. You will want to add toothpaste to whatever brush you choose. Your veterinarian will be able to recommend a suitable toothpaste.

Helpful hint: Never use human toothpaste on your dog's teeth. The foaming agent it contains can cause gastric problems in dogs. Avoid using baking soda or salt to clean your dog's teeth. They do not remove plaque effectively, and they contain sodium, which can be harmful to older dogs with heart disease.

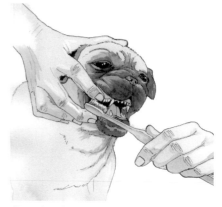

If you brush your pug's teeth regularly, poor dental hygiene will not put the bite on your pug's health.

Medicating and Feeding a Sick Pug

Ignorance is bliss when medicating a pug. As long as the pug remains ignorant of the contents of the mound of baby food you offer on a tablespoon or on the tips of your fingers, the pill hidden in that mound of food should go down easily. If your pug is too sick to eat, pills may have to be administered manually or with a pill gun. The latter is available in a pet shop or from a pet-supply catalog (see "Useful Addresses and Literature," page 92). Either way the technique is the same: Place the pill as far back on your pug's tongue as possible, hold his mouth shut, and stroke his throat until he swallows. Do not forget to praise him when he does.

Pugs convalescing from an illness or injury must consume enough fluid to replace that which they lose through elimination and panting. If your pug is unwilling to drink, you will have to get nourishing liquids—water or broths— down his throat one way or another.

Spooning fluid into a pug's mouth can be messy and uncomfortable for you and your dog. A syringe or a spray bottle is a better choice. Your veterinarian can tell you how much fluid your pug should receive daily.

If your pug is off his feed, switch to an all-canned-food diet and warm the food slightly in the microwave to release its aroma before giving it to him. Be sure to stir the warmed food and to test it for pockets of heat before offering it to your pug.

When a pug is not eating, virtually any food is nutritious food for the time being. Baby food, turkey or chicken from the deli, canned dog food marinated in beef or chicken broth, hamburger seasoned with garlic, broth straight up, anything that will revive your pug's interest in eating. (In serious cases you may have to feed your pug a pureed diet with a large syringe.)

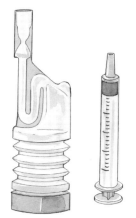

The bazooka-like pill "gun" (left) can be used to deliver a pill into a reluctant pug's mouth. The syringe (right) is used for feeding a sick pug.

Exercise

Pugs, being the civilized creatures they are, do not require much exercise. They like being outdoors, however, and if at all possible should be pro-vided with a securely fenced yard in which they can race about when the spirit moves them. They need not spend long amounts of time in the yard. An hour in the morning and another in the afternoon, weather permitting (and with access to fresh water, of course), are sufficient. Pugs that live in houses or apartments without yards should be walked 15 or 20 minutes at least once a day—this is in addition to their constitutional walks—and should be taken two or three times a week to an area where they can enjoy a good run under their owners' supervision.

Gifts often come with strings attached, and the pug's modest exercise needs are a case in point. Hot or humid weather are a challenge to a pug's respiration system, which has been compromised rather severely for the sake of a short nose. Pug owners, therefore, should have an accurate outdoor thermometer mounted somewhere near the yard. When the temperature reaches 80°F (27°C), do not leave your pug outdoors for more than five or ten minutes. To do otherwise is to court heatstroke.

Heatstroke, which occurs when rectal temperature spikes to 109.4°F (43°C) or when it lingers around 106°F (41°C), destroys cell membranes and leads to organ failures. The dehydration which accompanies heatstroke

Although they are not built for speed, pugs are surprisingly fast over short distances, achieving a high RPL (revolutions per leg) that carries them along nicely.

thickens the blood, which deprives tissues of necessary oxygen. The muscles, kidneys, liver, and gastrointestinal tract also may be affected. Moreover, heatstroke can cause swelling and subsequent damage to the brain, blindness, hemorrhages, convulsions, and fatal seizures.

If your pug becomes overheated and pants excessively after being outdoors, take his temperature at once. If his temperature is elevated, give him some cold water to drink and then reduce his temperature slowly with a cold-water bath.

Inherited Problems in Pugs

Like all pedigreed dogs, pugs are subject to a number of inherited disease conditions. The following are the ones most frequently encountered.

Legg-Perthes is a degeneration of the head of the femur bone, the long upper bone of the hind leg. Legg-Perthes occurs when the blood vessels supplying the head of the femur, which fits into the hip socket, do not grow and, therefore, do not carry

enough blood to the femoral head. As a consequence, the femoral head ceases to grow and eventually begins to disintegrate, affecting a pug's gait and causing him considerable pain. Legg-Perthes usually occurs before a pug is ten months old. Anyone who acquires a pug before he reaches that age should have the pug x-rayed at about ten months. Legg-Perthes can be corrected by surgery.

Luxating patella is a dislocation of the patella, the small, flat, moveable bone at the front of the knee. In mild cases the patella, which is held in place by ligaments, pops out of the groove in the femur in which it normally resides, then pops back in of its own accord. In severe cases the patella cannot return to its correct position on its own, and when it is manipulated into place, does not remain there long. A pug with luxating patella favors his affected leg when he walks, and when he runs, he lifts it, setting it down only every few steps.

The tendency to luxating patella is inherited, but excess weight can aggravate the tendency. Luxating patella can be corrected by surgery.

Pug-dog encephalitis is an inflammation of the brain that is unique to pugs. The cause has not been identified.

Seizure is the primary symptom of pug-dog encephalitis, which tends to affect young to middle-aged pugs. Seizures are sometimes preceded by periods of lethargy and loss of muscle coordination. Other signs include agitation, aggression, pacing in circles, and pressing the head against objects.

Pugs with the slow, progressive form of encephalitis will return to normal between seizures, which will reoccur in a few days to a few weeks. Pugs with the acute, rapidly progressing form of the disease walk abnormally and appear depressed and bewildered between seizures.

The pug's
skeletal structure:
1. *lower jaw*
   (mandible)
2. *skull*
3. *cervical vertebrae*
4. *thoracic vertebrae*
5. *lumbar vertebrae*
6. *tail vertebrae*
7. *pelvis*
8. *hip joint*
9. *femur*
10. *knee joint (stifle)*
11. *tibia and fibula*
12. *hock (tarsas)*
13. *metatarsals*
14. *metacarpals*
15. *radius and ulna*
16. *elbow*
17. *humerus*
18. *shoulder joint*

Phenobarbital helps to control seizures; corticosteroids help to reduce the inflammation of the brain; antibiotics can provide some relief if there is a bacterial component to the disease, but there is no cure for pug-dog encephalitis.

Progressive retinal atrophy (PRA) is the wasting away of the vessels in the retina, the innermost coat of the posterior part of the eyeball. PRA is manifest initially as night blindness in young dogs. As the disease progresses, its victims become totally blind.

Entropion is an inversion of the eyelid that usually affects the lower lid. Entropion, which can be corrected by surgery, causes persistent irritation of the cornea.

Pigmentary keratitis is the deposition of pigment or melanin on the surface of the eye by the cornea in response to unrelieved irritation and/or inflammation. Pigmentary keratitis is nature's way of telling pug breeders they have gone too far in their quest for facial extremity, for as breeders have shortened the pug's muzzle, they also have created the pug's excessive nasal folds and shallow eye sockets. The latter cause the eyes to protrude, and if they protrude over-much, the eyelids cannot fully cover and protect the cornea, nor can they distribute the tear film effectively over the entire surface of the eye. This condition is known as lagophthalmos, and it is one of the causes of pro-lapsed eyes and of dry eye or kerato-conjunctivitis (KCS). Other irritating factors include ingrown eyelashes (trichiasis), aberrant eyelid hairs (distichiasis), and trauma to the eye.

Pigmentary keratitis can be permanent if the cause of the irritation or inflammation is not removed—by surgery, if necessary—be it excessive nasal fold tissue, ingrown hairs, or KCS. After the cause of the problem has been eliminated, superficial deposits of pigment can be treated with topical eye medications. Pigment deep within the cornea may not be so easily treated, and if it impairs a pug's vision, it should be removed surgically.

Elongated soft palate, which occurs in pugs and other short-faced breeds like the bulldog and the Pekingese, often results in some degree of obstruction of the dog's airway. This obstruction results in snorting, snoring, and breathing through the mouth. In severe cases of elongated palate, the palate partially blocks the opening into the voice box. If secondary changes in the voice box take place, acute airway obstruction may occur. If your pug begins to honk like a goose, put his head back, and gasp for air, consult your veterinarian to see if he or she considers your pug a candidate for the surgery necessary to correct an elongated soft palate.

Stenotic nares, a birth defect found in short-nosed breeds, is caused by nasal cartilage that is too soft. Stenotic nares, literally "narrow nostrils," collapse when a dog inhales, thereby preventing the dog from drawing in air. Dogs with this condition have a foamy-looking nasal discharge, and they breathe through their mouths when excited. Stenotic nares can be corrected surgically.

It goes without saying, which is why it needs to be said, that sensible breeders will not use pugs suffering from any inherited defect in their breeding programs. In pugs, as in all breeds, the dramatic is shadowed closely by the detrimental.

Because not all breeders are as conscientious as they should be, persons acquiring a pug should ask the seller who will be responsible for the vet bills if a pug should be victimized by an obviously inherited condition later in life.

Understanding Your Pug

There is no better company on two legs or four than a pug dog. No friend is more loyal, no comrade more jolly, no confidant more trusty than this snuffling little bundle of *joie de vivre*.

If pugs had their way—and every pug should—they never would be more than an arm's length from their owners. As this is being written, four pugs are camped in their cuddle beds on the office floor. If I go to the kitchen to make coffee, the pugs will follow. If the phone rings—as it always does as soon as I leave the office—and I go back to the office to answer it, the pugs will tag along. When I return to the kitchen to finish making coffee, the pugs will fall into line. When I get my car keys before going to the post office, the pugs will race to the kitchen door and look at me as if to say, "Where are we going now?" And so it goes throughout the day until it is time to retire—with a quartet of pugs to anchor the quilt.

A house is not a home without two or three cuddle beds for your two or three pugs to occupy as they follow you from room to room throughout the day.

The Adaptable Pug

Pugs are willing to hold court in town or country. Their spirit can warm a drafty old mansion. Their simple requirements can be accommodated in the tiniest flat. Fame, wealth, power, accomplishment, or social status make no difference to pugs. Home is where the heart is, and their hearts are with their masters.

In addition to the unflagging companionship they provide, there are practical advantages to owning pugs. They travel more easily and are accepted more readily in hotels or motels than are larger breeds. Pugs will not eat a hole in your discretionary income. They do not require a lot of exercise. They can be

Anyone who could resist such a face would have to be impervious to cute.

washed quickly and allowed to drip dry, and best of all, because they are small you can have more than one.

Multum in Parvo

Such is the pug's zest for living that the breed has been accorded its own motto: *Multum in parvo,* a Latin expression that means "a lot of dog in a small space." No one knows at what point in its 2,500-year history the pug acquired this motto, but its author knew whereof he or she was speaking. The pug dog is, indeed, larger than life.

A pug gives you the convenience of a toy breed, the heart of a giant, the bravery of a terrier, the intelligence of a herding dog, and the face of a clown. Pugs are as loving, constant, and devoted as the day is long, as dependable as the sunrise. They are the best medicine when you are sick, an antidote to sadness when you are well, and the greatest conversation starters on four feet. Most of the time the conversations begin favorably with some variation on the "My, what cute little dogs" theme, but one chap, more candid than cautious, said to me outside a convenience store one day, "No offense, man, but those are some seriously ugly dogs." He was smiling, however, when he said it.

The other misperception often expressed by the uninitiated is that pugs, because of their size, are somehow wimpy or, worse yet, wimp's dogs. My friend John, who favors trucks and hunting breeds, sneeringly referred to our pugs as fake-a-dogs after we had gotten them. When we had only two pugs, John often suggested that we "trade 'em both in and get a real dog."

One Saturday night in early spring we took our pugs with us to John's for a visit. Percy, our neutered male whose name did nothing to alter John's opinion of small dogs, took up residence near the rocking chair in which John was sitting. As the evening and the conversation progressed, no one paid much attention to Percy except to comment from time to time on his sonorous snoring.

Perhaps in a gesture of conciliation, John reached down, put his hand on Percy's neck, and while moving his hand back and forth somewhat briskly said, "What do you say, Percy?"

What Percy said cannot be recorded in a book intended for a family audience. It may have sounded like a growl to the others in the room, but I recognized a series of hyphens joining several of the words in that growl.

More than what Percy said, it was what he did that stays in my mind and still elicits a chuckle today. While John's hand was still on Percy's shoulder, the little gent leaped to his feet smartly, spun around, growled his hyphenated growl, then stood on his hind legs, put his front legs on the seat of John's rocker, and stared straight ahead menacingly.

By this time John's hands were up in the air as though Percy were threatening his life, which in a sense Percy was. There was no place for John to go, and nothing for him to say but, "Hey, Percy, take it easy."

Thinking gleefully to myself, "Every dog has his day," I called Percy over to me, and the rest of the evening passed without incident.

Pugs may not stand over a lot of ground, but they are always ready to defend their turf.

A Trace of Determination

Although pugs are the most devoted of companions, they sometimes are determined to have their way. We learned this one April when our female Debbie had her first litter.

There were three puppies in Debbie's litter. Two survived, the second of those only through the diligence of our vet, who popped over at 4:00 A.M. to coax out the reluctant puppy and to shake the life into her. Afterwards, we put Debbie and her girls into the whelping box and put our tired selves into bed.

Immediately we heard a piteous mewling and an indignant snort. My wife Mary Ann turned on the light. Peering accusingly over the top of the whelping box were Debbie's large, luminous eyes. They clearly said, "Have you forgotten that I sleep with you guys? Why have you shut me in here with these dwarfs? What do they want from me?"

We told her it was not unusual for puppies to expect maternal attention. She replied with a phrase that not even the censors on "In Living Color" would approve.

We tried sleeping with our backs to the whelping box. We wondered where we might find ear plugs at 6:00 A.M. We hand-fed the puppies at 6:30 A.M. A few of our retired mother cats grumbled disapprovingly in the hallway.

Two of the author's pugs racing as fast as their short legs will carry them, trying to keep up with Leviathan, the Doberman next door, who has barely broken into a lope.

Like stranded travelers in the desert who think they see an oasis, I thought I saw Debbie allowing her puppies to nurse several times throughout the morning. Mary Ann had gone off to teach on no sleep. Feeling somewhat guilty, but not guilty enough to stop, I lay down to take a nap around midafternoon. Debbie insisted on joining me. I was about halfway to REM sleep when I heard mewling. I glanced at the clock. It was 3:00 P.M. The next thing I knew it was 3:45 P.M. The puppies were still mewling. Debbie was sound asleep. I knew what T. S. Eliot meant when he said that April is the cruelest month.

Since Debbie no more wanted to stay in the whelping box than walk on hot coals—and since we were afraid she might step on a puppy while she was hopping up and down to protest her captivity—we struck a bargain. The poor, abandoned puppies would sleep alone on their heating pad in the whelping box if Debbie would agree to let them nurse from her on the bed at the proper intervals. We, of course, would have to get up at those proper intervals around the clock to oversee this arrangement.

Debbie tentatively agreed, pending approval from her shop steward. After a week we no longer had to hold her down while her puppies nursed. After two weeks she began to take an interest in cleaning them. We do not approve of factory-farming, but we were tempted to trade the whelping box for one of those restraining devices into which pig farmers lock their sows.

Debbie's girls are grown now. Indeed, one has puppies of her own. Fortunately, she was the textbook mother, a triumph of instinct over example. And guess who is the picture of grandmotherly solicitude, sitting with all six of her grandkids arranged adoringly about her? Yep, Old Deb. That is a pug for you.

Comic Relief

A pug is a punch line in search of a laugh. This dichotomy in fur possesses a body that looks like a cookie jar and a gentle, jolly disposition belied by a face that appears as if its owner has just received tragic news. Thus, the more pugs try to be serious, the funnier they become.

Our pugs are seldom more amusing than when they try to match strides with the Doberman next door. At least once a day his owners take him outside and throw or bat a ball for him to chase. The Doberman goes after the ball in graceful, loping strides—poetry in motion, a lesser writer might say.

Meanwhile, on their side of the chain-link fence, our four pugs are hurtling along helter-skelter, legs a-blur, eyes a-bulge, ears a-flapping. Our fence ends before the Doberman's yard does, and he has picked up the ball and is loping back to his owner by the time our pugs reach the end of the fence. Like characters in a cartoon, they put on the brakes, do a U-turn, spin their wheels for a split second before getting traction, and race back to where the Doberman's owner has just hit the ball again. On go the brakes, the last pug becomes first, and the pugs are off again. If the Doberman's owner stops to pet him before throwing the ball, our pugs start hopping up and down like automated pogo sticks, barking their heads off, their loose skin piled like a dropped pair of drawers around their butts.

Soon after we had gotten our pugs we stopped going to restaurants that did not have windows near which we could sit, the better to keep an eye on the dogs, who insist on going everywhere that we go and who look at us as though we were child abusers if we try to leave the house without them. One afternoon while I was enjoying a few slices of pizza and *The Spectator* in a local establishment, I heard a horn being sounded somewhat impatiently. A few seconds later I heard it again. Then again.

"I think your dogs are calling you," said the pizza-shop owner's wife, who was fairly doubled over with laughter.

When I looked out the window, I saw why. There was Patty, front paws on the steering wheel of the minivan, looking for all the world like an irate driver stuck in some surrealistic traffic jam, her head bobbing up and down while she barked insults at the world. In the other front seat, equally frosty-looking, sat her mother, Debbie, with a thousand-yard glare on her face. When Patty finally stopped tooting the horn and the owner of the pizza shop finally stopped laughing, the minivan lights came on. It was time to go home.

Anyone writing a book about pugs would run out of space long before running out of anecdotes, for pugs are endlessly amusing. Through the centuries they have been bred for one purpose alone: to provide love and companionship to a species that desperately needs them. Pugs are good at their work, so good, in fact, that a friend of ours is fond of saying, "A dog is a dog, but a pug is another person in your house." And what good people they are. A house is not a home without a pug.

Patty, signaling a left-hand turn and keeping her right foot on the horn, takes her eyes off the road momentarily while she waits for the author to emerge from the pizza shop.

Two for the Shows

In 1877 the Westminster Kennel Club presented the first dog show in the United States. Thirty-five breeds competed. Seven years later there was enough interest in showing dogs in this country to warrant the formation of the American Kennel Club (AKC). Today the AKC recognizes 136 breeds and sanctions roughly 10,000 events annually, including conformation shows, obedience trials, and field trials. Many of these events are advertised in dog magazines. If there is no dog magazine available at your newsstand, call one of their subscription departments (see "Useful Addresses and Literature," page 92) and ask to buy the latest issue. Newspapers also may contain notices for local shows in the "Pets" section of the classified ads or in the notices of coming events in the "Living," "Life-style," or "Weekend" sections.

The Premium List, Entry Form, and Confirmation

A premium list contains both information about a scheduled show and the entry form necessary for entering dogs in that show. Premium lists publish the date and location of the show, the names of the judges for every breed eligible to compete in the show, directions to the show site, information relating to overnight camping facilities, the date on which entry forms are due at the superintendent's office, and lists of special prizes being offered at the show.

A premium list may be obtained from the show superintendent. A roster of superintendents is printed each month in *Dog World* magazine and in the *Events Calendar,* published by the AKC. To obtain premium lists for shows in your area, write to one or two superintendents and ask to be put on their mailing lists.

Once an entry form is completed, the exhibitor mails it with the appropriate fee or faxes it to the show superintendent. Faxed entries are charged to the exhibitor's credit card. Entries generally cost between $15 and $20, and they are usually due at the superintendent's office 18 days or so before the day of a show.

About one week before the show, exhibitors receive a confirmation packet from the superintendent. That packet contains an entry card, a judging schedule, the number of entries for each breed, and the numbers of the rings in which the various breeds will be judged. The entry confirmation also contains a facsimile of a dog's listing in the show catalog.

Helpful hint: Check the facsimile of your dog's catalog listing carefully to make sure all names are spelled correctly, the dog's registration number is accurate, and the dog has been entered in the correct class. Errors should be reported to the superintendent as soon as an exhibitor reaches the show.

Varieties of Competition

In conformation shows, which are open to unaltered dogs only, contestants are judged against a written standard. In obedience trials, in which neutered males and spayed bitches also may compete, contestants are judged on their ability to obey specific commands. Field trials, which are held separately for basset hounds, beagles, dachshunds, pointing breeds, retrievers, and English springer spaniels, are designed to test the capacity of a dog to perform the task for which its breed was created. Titles are awarded to successful dogs that meet established criteria in each type of competition.

Types of Shows

Pug owners who want to enter their dogs in conformation or obedience shows can choose among four types of events: the match show, the all-breed show, the specialty show, and the group show. The latter three shows are also known as point shows because dogs and bitches competing in them may win points toward championship or obedience titles.

Match Shows

Match shows offer inexperienced exhibitors or their dogs a chance to become ringwise in a relaxed setting. Although match shows are similar to point shows, no points toward championships or other titles are awarded at match shows, nor do match-show judges need to be licensed by the AKC. What's more, puppies as young as three months of age may be entered in a match show. (At point shows puppies must be at least six months old in order to compete.)

All-breed Shows

These are AKC-licensed shows at which all 136 breeds recognized for championship competition are eligible to compete for points toward their championship or obedience titles. Entries at all-breed shows regularly exceed 1,000, and shows with 2,000 entries or more are not uncommon.

Specialty Shows

These are AKC-licensed shows in which only one breed is eligible to compete for championship points and other awards. The Pug Dog Club of America holds a national specialty show each year. In addition, regional pug clubs hold their own specialty shows throughout the year.

The pug, says the AKC standard, "is an even-tempered breed, exhibiting stability, playfulness, great charm, dignity, and an outgoing, loving disposition."

Group Shows

These are AKC-licensed shows held for the breeds that belong to any of the seven groups into which pedigreed dogs are classified. Pugs, which belong to the toy group, would compete in shows held only for members of that group.

A Word About Judging Conformation Shows

The majority of pugs compete in conformation shows, which actress and dog-lover Mary Tyler Moore has described as "nonsexist beauty pageants." Winners in the different classes offered at conformation shows are decided in an altogether subjective manner. Judges of varying degrees of competence and familiarity with a breed evaluate each entry in a class according to a written standard for that breed. Because breed standards are constructed broadly enough to allow men and women of good will to interpret them differently, a dog that was best in show on Friday might not even be best in its breed at the following day's show. Indeed, one dog-show judge and breeder has written that the continuing success of the dog fancy is predicated to an extent on inconsistent judging, otherwise the same dogs would win all the time and few people would bother to enter their dogs in shows.

In conformation shows, males (which are called dogs) and females (which are called by the unfortunate-sounding term, bitches) are competing for points that will make them champions. They also are competing for best-of-breed, best-in-group, and best-in-show awards.

A dog or a bitch must earn 15 points to become a champion. Those points can be earned one, two, three, four, or five at a time, depending on the number of other entries a dog or a bitch defeats in competition. Before explaining what distinguishes a one-from a two- from a five-point win, we should describe the kinds of classes offered at all-breed, specialty, and group shows.

Which Class to Enter?

All dogs and bitches that have not earned their championships compete against other nonchampion members of their breed and sex for points toward championship. Nonchampion dogs or bitches, known as class dogs or class bitches, may be entered in one of the first five classes described below:

Puppy, for entries between 6 months and one day under 12 months of age. Sometimes the puppy class is divided into a puppy 6-to-under-9-month class and a puppy 9-to-under-12-month class. In addition, classes for dogs and bitches 12 to under 18 months old are offered at all shows.

Novice, for entries that have never earned a first-place ribbon in any class. After a dog or bitch has earned three first-place ribbons, it must be entered in one of the other classes at subsequent shows.

Bred by exhibitor, for entries six months and above that are being shown by persons who bred and currently own or co-own them.

American bred, for entries six months and above that were bred in the United States.

Open, for entries six months and above.

Winners, for the winners of each of the five classes described above. This class is held immediately after the preceding five classes have been judged.

The Mechanics of Judging

Nonchampion (or class) dogs are judged before nonchampion (or class) bitches. In each class the judge awards first- through fourth-place ribbons if the size and quality of the class warrant them. After all classes have been judged, winning dogs from the various classes return to the ring immediately for the winners class. The winner of that class—that is, the winner's dog—receives points toward the champion title. (Class bitches are judged in the same sequence as class dogs, and the winners bitch is chosen in the same fashion.)

At a few shows there is also a class for veteran dogs. The age limits for this class vary.

After the veteran's class has been judged, the best-of-breed class is held. This class is for champions (also known as specials) of both sexes and for the winners dog, the winners bitch, and the winner of the veteran's class. In the best-of-breed class, all dogs and bitches compete for best of breed and best of opposite sex to best of breed. In addition, the winners dog and the winners bitch compete for the best-of-winners ribbon.

At specialty shows the competition is over at this point. In group and all-breed shows, best-of-breed winners return later in the day to compete in their respective groups. The best-of-breed pug competes in the toy group. Other groups are the sporting, hound, working, terrier, nonsporting, and herding.

Judges award first- through fourth-place ribbons in group competition. At group shows the competition is over at this point, but in all-breed shows, the seven group winners compete for best in show at the end of the day.

Counting up the Points

The number of points earned by the winners dog and the winners bitch are determined by the number of other class entries those winners defeat. During the 1993 show season in Division 2 of the AKC, a division that comprises Delaware, New Jersey,

Because black is dominant in pugs, at least half the puppies in a litter will be black, on average, in breedings between a black and a fawn pug.

Pennsylvania, and Ohio, two class (or nonchampion) pug dogs present and competing constituted a one-point show. Five class dogs present and competing constituted a two-point show. Nine dogs constituted a three-point show; 13 dogs a four-point show; and 19 or more a five-point show. In bitches, two entries were required for a one-point show; six for a two-point show; 11 for a three-point show; 16 for a four-point show; and 25 or more for a five-point show. No dog or bitch can earn more than five points at a time toward championship, no matter how many entries are defeated.

The number of entries needed for a one-, two-, three-, four-, or five-point show is based on the number of pugs of each sex that competed in a region during the preceding show season. Requirements may change from one region to the next, from one season to the next, and from one breed to the next.

All 15 points needed to become a conformation champion may not be accumulated one or two at a time, however. Two wins must be major wins—that is, wins that are worth three, four, or five points. And those major wins must come from two different judges.

Mathematically, the fastest a dog or a bitch can finish a championship is in three shows. In actuality it takes more shows than that—a lot more for the majority of champions. Fifteen to 30 shows on average, and sometimes beyond.

Ring Procedure

Upon entering the ring, exhibitors line up their dogs or bitches down one side of the ring or, if the class is large, down two or more sides. Exhibitors then stack their dogs (see "Stacking," page 68) while the judge walks down the line taking a first-impression look at the entries in the class.

The judge then asks the exhibitors to walk their dogs around the ring in a circle en masse. After the exhibitors come to a halt, the judge inspects each entry individually. Pugs and other small breeds are examined on a table.

After the judge has examined an entry, he or she asks the exhibitor to gait (or walk) the dog in one or two patterns (see "Gaiting Patterns," page 67). Finally, after the judge has inspected every entry in a class, he or she may ask a few individuals to gait their entries again, or else the judge may simply ask the entire class to circle the ring. At that juncture the judge will point to the first-, second-, third-, and fourth-place finishers in the class. These dogs and their exhibitors line up to receive their ribbons while the rest of the class leaves the ring. (In best-of-breed classes, the judge will indicate a maximum of three winners: best of breed, best of opposite sex, and best of winners.)

Practicing at Home

For manners' and for safety's sake, the diligent pug owner teaches his or her pug to walk on a lead (see page 28). The diligent exhibitor will want to refine that ability—and the lead itself if it is too thick or clunky-looking—for the show ring. There a pug is expected to walk smartly at the exhibitor's left side, neither lagging behind nor running in front.

Gaiting Patterns

Exhibitors usually are asked to gait their dogs or bitches in one or more of three patterns: the circle, the down-and-back, and the triangle. The patterns should be practiced at home until pug and exhibitor are stepping along handsomely.

All an exhibitor needs for a basic practice session are a willing pug, a lead, a 40 × 50-foot (12 × 15 m) patch of yard, and some bait (either cooked liver or some other special-occasion treat). Extended sessions may involve a friend,

"It is difference of opinion that makes horse races," said Mark Twain. The same can be said about dog shows.

spouse, or housemate, another dog or two, and a public park. The extra dogs and the park are a way of getting a pug used to walking and ignoring other people and dogs at the same time.

The trick to showing dogs is to make it fun for them. Ideally, a pug should begin hopping around gleefully at the sight of a lead because the pug knows there are treats and a chance to be the center of attention forthcoming. Thus, each practice session should begin with a minute of two of copious petting and a few treats to get the pug's attention. Then, slip the lead on the dog and let the work begin.

Start with several down-and-backs. With the pug on the left, walk 15 or 20 feet (4.5–6. m), make a U-turn right, then walk back to the starting spot. Upon bringing the pug to a halt, reach into a pocket and take out a piece of bait. This will get the pug's attention, which is fine. Pugs are supposed to look fetchingly animated. If the bait gets the pug up on its hind legs, however, say "no" or "down" and make sure the pug has all four feet on the ground and is standing still for five or ten seconds before surrendering the treat.

Sitting down must be discouraged also. Whenever your pug sits, just say "no" and tug the lead gently until the dog stands up.

After several down-and-backs to limber dog and exhibitor, try a few circles with an eight- to ten-foot (2.43–3 m) radius. At the end of each circle, bring your pug to a halt, show the bait, and make sure your pug stands still for five to ten seconds before rewarding it.

Finally, practice the triangle pattern. Walk a 15 to 20 foot (4.5–6 m) straight line, turn left, go 10 to 15 feet (3–4.5 m), then come back to the starting point on the diagonal. Repeat the exhibitor-shows-bait, dog-stands-still routine at the end of each triangle.

Lead work need not last more than 15 or 20 minutes a day, every second

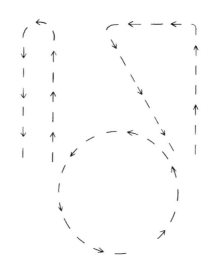

Before you take your pug to a show, practice walking these patterns with him until the two of you can walk them calmly and gracefully.

or third day, until a puppy gets the knack of walking correctly. If a puppy begins lead work at three or four months, practice sessions can be cut to twice a week once he is trained adequately. Some owners increase those sessions to three or four times a week a few weeks before a show.

In addition to teaching a pug good ring manners, lead training should develop the gaiting speed at which a pug looks most natural. Although pugs are supposed to be shown on a loose lead, that prescription is rarely observed. The tighter the exhibitor's nerves (or the more spirited the pug), the tighter the lead. But even united by a tight lead, pug and owner should look relaxed. There should be nothing of the forced march about this exercise. Nor should the owner look as if he or she is in a hurry to get to a rest room. One should walk in a graceful promenade, keeping one eye on the dog and the other on the judge, while striving to maintain a look of confident aplomb.

For his part, the pug should not be allowed to sniff the ground or to walk with his head drooping, which makes a dog's topline (the line from shoulder to tail) appear unlevel. If your pug begins sniffing or ducking his head, a short tug on the lead will bring his head to the desired position. Do not jerk the lead strongly. The idea is to get your dog's attention, not to lift him off his feet. The lead is a corrective, not a coercive, device.

Stacking

Stacking is the art of positioning a dog so as to accentuate his best qualities and minimize his flaws. Because pugs are examined on a table at shows, in addition to being stacked on the ground, they should be stacked on a table, on which a rubber mat has been placed, at home. The kitchen table or a picnic table in the yard are good stages on which to practice stacking.

With the lead on your dog, lift him to the table and loop the lead around your neck, thereby leaving your hands free. Position your pug, his face near your right hand, about one inch from the edge of the table. His front legs should be impeccably straight. Lift both front legs a few inches off the table and set them down in the

desired, straightforward position. If your pug tends to toe one front leg in or out, turn that leg to the desired position (always turn from the top, not the middle, of the leg) and set that leg in place first.

To position the rear legs, which should be slightly extended, first hold your left hand perpendicular to the table, fingers together, palm facing your pug's front, thumb up. Then slide your left hand under the dog, stopping right in front of his rear legs, and guide the rear legs back into the position in which you want them. The correct position should make your dog's top line look absolutely level.

When your pug is looking picture perfect, hold a piece of bait about a foot (30 cm) in front of his face, slightly above nose level. If your pug does not have as many wrinkles in his forehead as you would like, hold the bait a little lower and, grasping the lead a few inches (5 cm) from the pug's neck, pull the lead forward.

Feeding on the Day of a Show

Some owners and handlers insist that a pug should not be fed the morning of a show because "I want him (or her) looking at me in the ring." I have never followed this advice because I know how I would feel if I were obliged to go without breakfast just to go to a dog show. What's more, pugs are ever eager for a treat, even if they have eaten five minutes earlier, and they are so eager to please that they will show plenty of animation if we show them that that is what we want.

Do You Need a Handler?

Because handling a pug does not require as much fleetness of foot or deftness of comb as handling some other breeds requires, the majority of pugs are handled by the persons who bred them, and owner-handled pugs do quite well. What's more, doing it

A pug being stacked at home. Stacking is the art of positioning a dog in such a manner as to reflect its good points while concealing its defects from a legally sighted judge who is standing a short distance away.

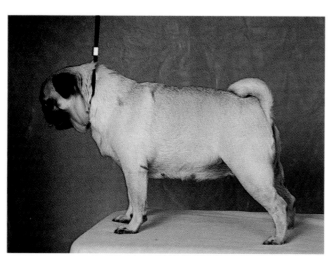

yourself is cheaper. Handlers charge $50 to $75 just to walk into the ring; and if they have to take your dog with them overnight, you will subsidize a portion of the handler's traveling, lodging, and eating expenses, too.

On the other hand, a professional knows tricks that a novice could be a long time learning, and a professional is known by more judges than a novice is. Finally, some owner-exhibitors show their pugs so often and are so well-known that showing against them is like showing against a professional anyway.

Determined do-it-themselfers will no doubt tough it out, take their lumps in the beginning, and eventually show their pugs to championships, if the pugs are sufficiently good and the owner is sufficiently determined. Persons with less motivation or ego needs (or more stage fright or discretionary income) will leave the walking to the professionals.

Provisions for a Show

The most important items to pack for a show are the entry card and show confirmation, the lead, some bait, a folding chair, and a spray bottle filled with water. (You will need the latter if your pug gets overheated.)

Even if you are showing a pug that is used to riding loose in the car and walking nonchalantly through crowds, and the weather is fine, you should take along a dog carrier or a folding crate—19 inches (48 cm) wide, 24 inches (61 cm) long, and 21 inches (53 cm) high. Also, pack two towels, one for the inside of the carrier or crate and one for the top. If you are showing by yourself, a carrier is more convenient for transporting your pug to the ring if the weather turns wet or the show ground is soggy or dusty. In any case, a wooden platform with wheels will make it easier to get a crate to the ring.

The incidental items packed for a show are determined by personal comfort. Some exhibitors trundle off with enough provisions for a two-month stay in a biosphere. Others pack more conservatively.

Basic Show Supplies Checklist

- ☐ Flea comb
- ☐ Brush
- ☐ Cotton swabs
- ☐ Cotton balls
- ☐ Paper towels
- ☐ Facial tissues
- ☐ Washcloth
- ☐ Eye drops
- ☐ Pen
- ☐ Spray disinfectant
- ☐ Can opener
- ☐ Bottle opener
- ☐ First-aid kit
- ☐ Business cards
- ☐ Food
- ☐ Spoon
- ☐ Biodegradable paper plates
- ☐ Bottled water from home
- ☐ Water bowl
- ☐ Magazine or book
- ☐ Pooper scooper
- ☐ Small plastic baggies

Pugs are like a certain brand of potato chip: it is difficult to stop at just one.

Obedience Training

Despite their not entirely deserved reputation for being single-minded (some would say stubborn), pugs are apt and willing pupils, eager to please and able to learn. As your pug's teacher, you must bring the same cheerful, intelligent, resolute bearing to each training session. Because your patience will be tried and rewarded alternately while you are teaching your pug to come, sit, stay, and so on, do not begin training at the end of a frustrating day. The last thing you need at that point is another obstruction in the person of a recalcitrant pug who, purely out of spite and malice, of course, does not do what you want as soon as you want it.

Obviously, your pug does not refuse your petition out of spite or malice. Those are human qualities that humans project onto animals, especially when humans are keyed up because of something the boss, the clerk at the convenience store, the person in the next cubicle at work, the President, some editorial writer, a loved one, the neighbor's kid, or all of the above did or said recently. If your nose is out of joint, you should chop wood, go jogging, work out for half an hour, or put on your favorite album and the headphones. Leave the training for another day. All you need from your pug when you are cross is her nonjudgmental company while you sit and stare into space, brooding over the unfairness of it all.

When to Begin Training

Basic training, which essentially consists of teaching your pug where she should conduct her personal affairs, should begin as soon as you acquire your dog. As this training progresses, your pug will learn that certain behaviors are met with praise. The satisfaction your pug gets from being praised and her eagerness to please you are the foundations on which obedience training is built.

Most pugs are ready to start obedience training when they are six months old. Some may be ready a bit sooner; others later. Your knowledge of your pug's intelligence and maturity will help you to recognize when the time is right.

The Alpha-dog Principle

Dogs have always depended on the ability to function within a social hierarchy to survive, a dependence that leads them to seek our approval. In the wild—a concept that is difficult to entertain vis-à-vis pugs—dogs and their wolfish ancestors lived in a hierarchy dominated by the alpha member, or leader, of the pack. The alpha dog—who generally is, contrary to popular misperception, a female—is judge, jury, exalted ruler, and high priestess of the pack. When the alpha dog wants to rest, the other members of the pack lie down obligingly. When the alpha dog wants to move on, the pack follows. When the alpha dog wants to hunt, the pack members sharpen their fangs.

This centuries-old predisposition to function in a follow-the-leader arrangement makes it possible for you to assume the role of the alpha dog in your pug's life. This principle also

Training Tips

1. Keep training sessions brief: five minutes or so at a time, two or three times a day.

2. Conduct training sessions in the same location with the same unfailing patience each time. After your pug has mastered a command, you can vary the setting to see if that learning is transferable.

3. Reward your pug with praise and the occasional treat when she does well. If she associates performance with good feelings, she will be more likely to perform willingly.

4. Do not use your pug's name to scold her if she makes a mistake during training. In fact, do not scold your pug at all during training. When she makes a mistake, show her by voice and example what you want her to do.

5. Limit your pug to one teacher. Different people have different ways of interacting with dogs. This might be fine sociologically, but it plays havoc with the training experience.

6. If your pug attempts to leave before a training session is over, bring her back quietly and try again. Do not call her by name when you are trying to coax her back to the training site, or she might never come again when she is called.

7. Do not let the session end unless you are ready to end it.

8. If you are practicing indoors, have a lead handy in case the door-bell rings and you have to go and answer it in the middle of a training session. Put the lead on your pug and walk her to the door. Send the person away and go back to your training session. Of course you will not have to bother answering the phone during a training session. That is why answering machines were invented.

9. Let other members of the household know that you do not wish to be disturbed during a training session.

10. If your pug is not catching on to a lesson as quickly as you would like, ask yourself what you are doing wrong. Are you going too quickly? Are you handling your pug too abruptly? Has an impatient tone infiltrated your voice? Are you rewarding your pug as soon as she does the right thing? Is it time to take a step back and go over a routine she already knows for a few days in order to build up her confidence before coming back to the trick that is giving her trouble?

makes it possible for little 18-pound dogs to dominate people who are ten times their size—and who are often more intelligent to boot. Just as nature abhors a vacuum, pack animals abhor a democracy. Every pack must have a leader. If you do not want the job, your pug will gladly take it. Before you allow this to happen, you should remember the old saying to the effect that if you ain't the lead dog, the scenery seldom changes.

What's in a Name?

Some pug owners spend considerable time choosing their pugs' names. Other owners let names evolve out of the warp and woof of daily living. The latter kind of person usually has a dog named Trashmaster or Peabrain. Dogs belonging to people for whom names are a serious business usually answer to things like Waterford or Lord Halversham.

Our first pug, whom we acquired when he was nine months old, had

One of a pug's most endearing moves is the quizzical head ratchet, in which the head is turned from twelve o'clock to a few minutes before or after.

been named Percy before we got him. Because we live in a small town where anyone who goes out into the backyard and yells "Percy, come" at a small dog is liable to attract unfavorable attention from Peabrain's owners, we had planned to change Percy's name to something less conspicuous. Alas, by the time Percy arrived at our house, he had become attached to his name; and, as you no doubt recall from an earlier chapter, was quite fond of it. His name being the only thing he had brought with him from his former home, we decided not to change it. If your pug, no matter how old she is when you acquire her, has a name and knows what it is, we suggest you keep that name. You may shorten it some, if possible, for public consumption—from Percy to Perc with a soft "c," for example—but your pug will have enough to do adjusting to a new home without having to adjust to a new identity as well.

If your pug has not been named by her breeder, or if she has not yet

learned her name, you can teach her to respond to whatever name you want by rewarding her with extravagant praise every time she does.

Helpful hint: Like humans, dogs consider the sound of their names the world's sweetest music, and if that sound is associated with great praise, your pug will learn to respond to her name in short order.

Suppose, for example, you have decided to name your pug Bridget. While you are playing with her—or sitting quietly with her, for that matter—pronounce her name with a certain high-pitched, ascending gusto. If she looks in any direction but yours, do nothing. Wait a second or two and say her name again. Unless she is stone deaf, Bridget will look toward you eventually. When she does, say "Good!" and reward her with a torrent of pets, hugs, and kisses.

You have Bridget's attention now. Wait a minute or two and say her name again. You may have to say it once or twice or even three times, but if you put enough excitement into your tone, Bridget will look at you eventually. When she does, make a fuss over her again. After Bridget has responded to her name three or four times in one session, you have accomplished your mission. If you repeat that mission two or three times a day for a week or so, you will have Bridget's attention any time you call her name, and Bridget will come to realize that the sound of those two syllables has a special meaning all its—and her—own.

A Handful of Useful Commands

Come

The first command you should teach your pug is to come when she is called. Once she has learned to respond to a vocal summons virtually without fail or insubordination, you will have established a significant measure of control

72

over her, a control that could serve her well in times of trouble. What's more, the confidence you will have acquired in teaching your pug to come when you call, will give you more confidence in teaching her additional commands.

If Bridget is responding well to her name, teaching her to come when you call should not be difficult. Many dogs begin loitering in the kitchen well before mealtime. When they see the food bowl descending toward the floor, they zoom toward it instantly. You can make this tendency work to your advantage by saying "Bridget, come," before moving the bowl from the kitchen counter to the floor. (You could use "here" or any other word instead of "come" when you wish to summon Bridget, but once you have chosen a call word, use it exclusively.) It does not matter how old Bridget is when you begin this routine, but the best time to begin it is right after she has learned to respond to her name.

In addition to rewarding Bridget with her meal for coming when you call, be sure to add a lavish helping of praise before you set the bowl down. This will reinforce the behavior you desire

Time out and tongue out. Buster rests for a moment, still guarding his ball.

because Bridget will associate the word "come" with food and praise.

Some dogs do not appear in the kitchen until they hear the rattle of the dry-food container, the sound of a can being opened, or the sound of the drawer where the can opener is kept being opened. If Bridget is one of those dogs, say "Bridget, come," before doing any of these guaranteed-to-get-her-attention activities.

After two or three weeks you will have "trained" Bridget to come when you call. At mealtimes. But no doubt there will be other times of the day and other parts of the house where you will want her to answer this command readily.

Begin this second phase of training (it will be the first phase for those rare dogs that do not race to the kitchen at the sound of the can opener) in a room from which there is no escape and no foolproof place for Bridget to hide. Wander into that room with a few of Bridget's favorite treats in your pocket. If Bridget begins to come over to greet you, say "Bridget, come" and take a treat out of your pocket. As soon as Bridget is close enough to get the treat, say "Good!" in a high-pitched, happy tone and reward her with the treat.

Should Bridget appear more interested in what she was doing before

The sound of a can of food being opened is the sound of music to a pug.

73

you came in than in coming over to greet you, move casually to a spot about two or three feet from her. Say "Bridget, come," then offer her the treat. If Bridget comes to you, say "Good" and give her the treat. If she ignores you, reach over quietly, pick her up, move her to you, praise her with pats and a hug—but not with the word "good"—and give her the treat. Save "good" for those occasions when Bridget has done the requested action.

Praising a dog that has just ignored you might seem unwise, but you would be even less wise to allow Bridget to ignore you when she pleases. By picking Bridget up and moving her to the place where you want her to be, you are teaching her that she is either going to come when she is called or you are going to see that she does.

After Bridget has complied with the "come" command two or three times—willingly or by proxy—end the lesson. In this as in all other lessons, never end the lesson on a disobedient note. The last request you make of your dog must be obeyed, even if you have to fake obedience by carrying or walking her through the command.

Once Bridget begins to respond regularly to the "come" command, do not give her a food reward every time she comes when you call. If she knows she can get a treat every time, she may decide on occasion that it is more rewarding to continue what she was doing, even if she was doing nothing, than to get that old predictable treat. But if she does not get a treat every time, she will not be certain that treats are always forthcoming. Thus, she will be more likely to answer every time because she always will be hoping, as the old joke goes, that tonight is the night.

Psychologists call this maybe-yes, maybe-no technique "intermittent reinforcement." They caution, however, that the schedule of intermittent reinforce-

ment must not be predictable. If you withhold the treat every third time you summon Bridget, she will soon catch on to that fact and begin timing her refusals to coincide with the empty hand. To be effective, intermittent reinforcement must be random. If your training sessions consist of four or five practices of the "come" command during three or four sessions a day, withhold the treat the second time you call Bridget during the first session, the fourth time during the second session, and so on.

Do not be intermittent with your praise, however. You do not want Bridget thinking that you love her less for some performances than for others. Every time she comes when you call, say "Good," even if you do not give her a treat.

Repeat the "come" exercise a few times a day, limiting the distance Bridget has to travel to three or four feet and restricting each session to two or three minutes in which Bridget has answered your call three or four times. After Bridget is coming to you consistently when you call, increase the distance between the two of you by gradual increments: first, to four or five feet for several days and then to six or seven feet for several days. Keep increasing the distance between Bridget and you until she responds to your command from across the room.

Finally, if you want to impress yourself, call her from the next room. For obvious reasons, the best room for you to be in when you first attempt this feat is the kitchen. And the best thing to do right after you call her, providing she is an only child, is to rattle a box of dry food. (If you have other dogs, the sound of the dry-food box might draw a crowd, which would be counterproductive. Either put them in the yard when you are training Bridget or rely on your seductive voice alone.)

After Bridget is bounding regularly into the kitchen in response to the dry-food box, call her without shaking the box, and give her copious applause and a treat when she comes running. Then, once she is racing to the kitchen in response to your voice alone, try calling her from other rooms in the house. If necessary, use the dry-food box as an auxiliary training aid at first.

If at any point Bridget does not respond to your vocal summons from another room, do not make an issue of it and do not repeat the command. Perhaps she did not hear you, and even if she did, the worst conclusion she will reach is that she can ignore you on occasion when you are not in the same room as she. Even in that event you will still be miles ahead of the game. Many dogs figure they can ignore their owners from any distance any time they choose.

If your dog is colossally inflexible and refuses to come when you call—and if you are just as inflexible in your desire to teach her to respond to this command—put a harness or collar on her and attach the six-foot training lead to it (see "Lead Training," page 29). Then say, "Bridget, come" and tug gently and briefly on the lead. If she does not respond to the call-tug summons, call her again and tug on the lead. If there is still no answer, pick her up and carry her to the spot from which you summoned her. Praise her lavishly but do not give her a treat. Then dismiss the class. Until she begins answering to "Bridget, come" with no more prompting than a short tug on the lead, you must end every lesson by carrying her into base.

Eventually, Bridget should begin responding to the "come" command with little more than a gentle tug on the lead by way of spiritual guidance. This is your signal to eliminate the tug after you have called her. If she responds to your voice only, her reward should be prodigious. If she is not yet voice activated, revert to tugging on the lead as a means of inspiring her to come when called.

Be careful not to allow the use of the lead to degenerate into a tug of war. If Bridget digs in her heels and refuses to budge, walk over to her, pick her up gently, and move her to the spot from which you first called her.

When that glorious day on which Bridget comes to you in response to your voice alone finally dawns, bask in the glory of several more of those days. Then try the exercise without the benefit of the lead. If Bridget ignores you, go back to the lead.

From your pug's point of view, there are only two reasons for coming when she is called: praise and food. Therefore, when you are training her to come when she is called, she always expects you to be happy that she responded. Consequently, you should never call her when you want to give her medication, reprimand her, or do anything else that might cause her discomfort. If she associates a summons with an unpleasant consequence, she will begin ignoring all summonses.

After your pug has learned to come faithfully when you call, you can reduce the lavish praise to a simple "good girl" or a pat on the head by way of intermittent reinforcement. Do not eliminate the reinforcement altogether or you risk eliminating your pug's willing response.

Sit

Teaching your pug to sit on command evolves easily as an extension of lead training (see page 29). After walking several paces with your pug on a lead at your left, stop and switch the lead to your right hand. Position your right hand above your pug's head, say "Sit," and pull up lightly on the lead. At the same time, place your left hand on your pug's rump and press down gently but firmly. Once

To teach your pug to sit, say "Bridget, sit," while tugging gently upward on her lead and pushing gently downward on her rump.

Stay

After your pug has mastered the "sit" command, you can begin teaching her to stay. With your pug in a sitting position on your left and the lead in your left hand, lean down and place your right hand—palm toward your dog—about six inches (15 cm) in front of her face. Say "Stay" and after you do, move slowly until you are facing your puppy and your right hand is held in front of her face as though you were a policeman stopping traffic. The lead still will be in your left hand at this point, so if your puppy begins to move toward you, repeat the "stay" command and pull the lead straight up gently.

After your pug has remained in position for five seconds or so, release her by calling her to you and praising her and giving her a treat if you wish. Then take up the lead, walk several paces, tell her to sit, and once she does, repeat the "stay" command. Practice this command three or four more times before you end the lesson. As you practice the "stay" command on subsequent days, slowly increase the amount of time your pug stays in place before you release her. Once she begins to master the command, you can practice it indoors. You can practice it while she is standing, too. As the practice sessions continue, you will not need to reinforce the "stay" command with your hand.

When your pug has mastered the "stay" command, you can begin to increase the distance between the two of you while she is staying in place. Give her the "stay" command, set the lead on the ground, and take a small step or two backward. Repeat the "stay" command, with the raised-hand signal for reinforcement if your pug looks as if she is about to move. Return her to the sitting position if she does move. After she has remained in place for ten or fifteen seconds or

your pug sits down, praise her quietly, but control your enthusiasm. You want her to remain sitting. If she stands up, repeat the "sit" command. If you use a food reward in teaching this command, present it below your pug's nose so that she can reach down for it without leaving the sitting position.

Once Bridget has been sitting for a few seconds, say "Bridget, come" and continue walking. After several paces, repeat the "sit" command. Do this another two or three times and end the lesson.

As you repeat the "sit" command on subsequent days, your pug should need less and less prompting from the touch of the lead on her neck and your hand on her rump. She has mastered the "sit" command when she can come to a stop and sit promptly when she hears the word "sit" while walking on a lead. At this point you do not have to transfer the lead from your left hand to your right any longer.

Helpful hint: Once your pug has mastered the "sit" command on a lead, you and she can practice sitting around the house. Call her to you and when she responds, say "Bridget, sit." If she hesitates, press down gently on her rump until she does, then praise her and give her a reward.

The hand signal is a crucial part of the lesson plan for teaching your pug to stay.

add the word "stay" until you get the message across. Because it may be important someday for your pug's own safety to assume the "down" position when you are a good distance away from her, use your voice more than your hands in teaching this exercise.

Once your pug moves promptly and obediently from the "stay" to the "down" position, try the exercise in an open space, using the sit-stay-down-stay sequence until she is responding to these commands smartly. Then move away from her and walk around her at varying distances, repeating "down" or "stay" as necessary. If ever she gets up before she is released, be sure to return her to the "down" position and hold her there until you are ready to release her. The teacher is the only one who gets to say "School's out."

however long you want her to remain in place, release her and praise her for being a good dog.

During the course of several training sessions gradually increase the distance between you and your pug to ten yards (9.1 meters). Then, instead of giving the "stay" command and backing away from your pug, give the command, turn around, walk ten paces, then turn and face her. If she has learned her lessons well, she ought to be sitting obediently in place. If she has followed you instead, repeat the exercise, but this time after giving the "stay" command, walk only one or two steps before turning and facing your pug.

Down

The "down" command is taught without benefit of a lead as an extension of "sit." Give your pug the "sit" and then the "stay" commands. Once she is in the "stay" position with you standing directly in front of her, press her shoulders down with one hand and slide her legs forward into the down position with the other hand. As you do, say "Down." If she tries to get up, repeat the down command and

At first you will have to show your pug what "down" means by sliding her front legs into the "down" position.

Should You Breed Your Pug?

Breeding a handsome, well-mannered pug is an achievement of which one can be proud. There is, however, a great responsibility attached to this undertaking. Nearly 3 million purebred puppies are born each year, and one quarter of the dogs destroyed in animal shelters for lack of good homes are purebred. Thus, the decision to bring more puppies into the world should not be made lightly; and for all but a few people it is not one that should be made or even contemplated.

First Considerations

Before you breed your pug, you should ask yourself why you want to do so. If your answers include winning fame and fortune in the dog world, perhaps you should consider a hobby that does not involve living creatures. Few breeders become overnight sensations; few litters are filled with nothing but show-quality puppies; and few people make money selling puppies. Indeed, making money is never a valid reason for breeding any animal.

If you are not certain you will make your puppies as happy as they make you—and that you can find homes for them that are as good as the one you will provide while they are in your care—then you should not set about making puppies at all. In fact, you should never produce a litter for which you do not have good homes already—or the unwavering intention of providing a good home, namely yours, for any puppy you cannot place. And do not include on your list of qualified prospective owners any family member or friend who says casually that he or she would love to have a puppy. Those are not promises, they are wishes; and wishes generally evaporate a few minutes after you ring someone up and say, "I've got that puppy you were looking for."

I expect that most readers are about to skip to another section of the book by now. If you are still with me, perhaps you are merely curious, or perhaps you are the rare individual who is responsible enough to be entrusted with the privilege of raising puppies. If so, there are two more things you need to understand: much can go wrong in a planned mating, and in the animal world anything that can go wrong generally will sooner or later.

The Female's Heat Cycle

A heat cycle or season, more properly called *estrus*, is a period of sexual receptivity that occurs in most mammalian females, dogs included. In the majority of female dogs, estrus (from the Greek word for "mad passion") first occurs between ten and fourteen months of age. Male dogs, which are said to be always in season, generally become sexually mature at about the same time.

A dark, bloody vaginal discharge accompanied by vulvar swelling is the first sign that a female dog is in season. You no doubt will notice bloodstains on your floors and carpets at about the same time male dogs in your neighborhood notice the scent of pheromones, chemical substances discharged from your pug girl's vulva and excreted in her urine. To be certain that no unexpected matings take place, never leave your soon-to-be-willing girl in the yard by herself after she has come into season, no matter how sturdy you think your fence is.

Females do not ovulate as soon as they come into season; nor are they willing to accept a male's advances even if he has tunneled under your fence. For the first six to nine days or so that they are in season—a period technically known as *proestrus*—females will be uncooperative or aggressive if a male attempts copulation.

A change in the color of vaginal discharge—from dark red to pinkish or watermelon—marks the advent of *standing heat* or true estrus, the second phase of the heat cycle. If a female is approached by a male during this phase of her cycle, which generally lasts six to twelve days, she will raise her tail, flag it

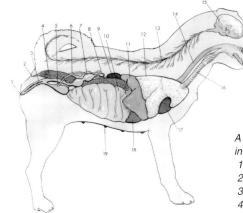

A female pug's internal organs:
1. vulva
2. anus
3. vagina
4. rectum
5. bladder
6. ureter
7. developing embryo
8. ovary
9. bladder
10. intestine
11. liver
12. lungs
13. spinal cord
14. trachea
15. brain
16. esophagus
17. heart
18. stomach
19. teat

to one side, lift her pelvis, present her vulva, and get a look on her face that clearly says, "Let the games begin."

When to Breed

Ovulation usually occurs some time during a female's standing heat, although it can occur in middle to late proestrus. Once the eggs are released from the ovary, they must mature roughly 72 hours before they are ready to be fertilized. After that they have only 48 to 72 hours to live. Fortunately, sperm can survive inside a female for up to seven days. Even more fortunately, blood tests can determine the optimum time for breeding a female. Your veterinarian should be able to tell you if there are reproductive specialists in your area who can administer these tests to your female. If there are no such wizards in your vicinity, perhaps your veterinarian can draw blood from your female and send it off to be analyzed, or perhaps your veterinarian will be able to tell from examining a vaginal smear when your female is ready to be bred. Failing this, too, breed on the tenth, twelfth, and fourteenth days from the first time you notice your girl is in heat. And count the day you first make this discovery as day one.

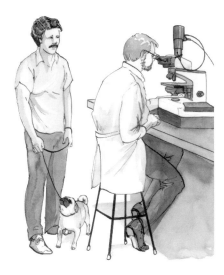

While a pug and her owner wait, a reproductive specialist studies a blood sample to determine the optimum day on which this pug should be bred.

Breed the Best to the Best

The Female
Only healthy, well-adjusted females that have been in season twice before, are 18 months of age, and are descended from forebears that have a history of trouble-free deliveries should be considered for breeding. And only those females whose pedigrees, conformation, and, in most cases, show records suggest that they have a contribution to make to their breeds should be considered seriously.

The Male
Selecting the right stud dog requires thought and investigation. Ample leads can be found by visiting dog shows to study the pugs being produced by today's studs and by reviewing back (and current) issues of *Pug Talk* (see "Useful Addresses and Literature," page 92).

In all this deliberation, the novice breeder should be guided by three principles: The stud dog should live in an antiseptically clean kennel; he should come from a family or a line of

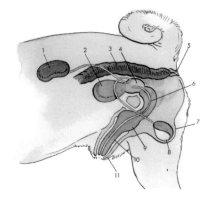

A male pug's urogenital organs.
1. kidneys 2. bladder 3. rectum 4. prostate
5. anus 6. urethra 7. scrotum 8. testes
9. bulb 10. penis 11. sheath

dogs that has crossed well with the female's line in the past; and he should be scrupulously efficient in producing those qualities the female lacks. If a female is light-boned, for example, there is little chance of producing heavier bone in her puppies if the male she is bred to has produced only fine- to medium-boned pups as a rule.

Pug puppies in a temporary state of rest that will be followed (and most likely has been preceded) by an ongoing state of play.

Genetics is so unpredictable that only the most carefully planned breedings have a better than random chance of producing top-quality pugs. In fact, the best a breeder can do in any breeding (ad)venture is to minimize the chances for failure. To achieve this end, many breeders prefer using an older stud dog, one who is already a grandfather, because it is easier to judge a male's reproductive potential by looking at his children and their children than by looking at the honors he has won.

Helpful hint: Too many people scurry off to breed to the latest winner, who may have proven himself in the show ring but who has yet to prove himself otherwise—and whose success may be more a function of style than of substance. This year's glamour pugs may develop into top producers one day, but for now it is more demonstrable that their fathers already have.

Contracts and Paperwork

Although they have little jurisdiction over a dog's genes, breeders can control the logistics of the mating process. No owner should take a female to a kennel to be bred unless the owner of that kennel is willing to provide a current health certificate for the stud dog in question. What's more, owners should be wary of sending their females to kennels that do not request the same certification for incoming females.

The stud-service contract is another document that should accompany all breeding arrangements. This contract does not have to be complicated or lengthy, but it should declare the fee involved, the responsibilities of the stud owner while the female is in his or her care, the length of time the stud owner is willing to keep the female, and the boarding fee, if any, that the stud owner charges for feeding and housing visiting females. The stud-service contract also should stipulate what happens if the female is mated but does not conceive; if she conceives but loses her puppies prematurely after she returns home; if she has only one live puppy; and any other eventuality that the parties to the contract consider important enough to put in writing.

Helpful hint: A stud-service contract, freely signed by two parties of sufficient age and mental capacity, is a legally binding document. Oral agreements are also legally binding, but (by definition) cannot be documented.

Pug puppies often put their heads together to plot their next act of mischief.

Whelping and Raising Puppies

The last eleven weeks of the writing of this book were graced and at times complicated by the presence, antics, and considerable demands of a litter of six pug puppies. We love them, and we will miss them terribly when they are gone, but after coping with that many puppies born at the beginning of one of the most grueling winters in recent memory on the East Coast, we have the following advice for anyone contemplating a December litter: Forget it. But if you must, be sure you have plenty of friends who read *The New York Times.* Its thick sections make the best floor covering for paper training.

Identifying Pregnancy

The first outward sign that a female is pregnant is a discreet swelling about the nipples. This enlargement, accompanied by a change in skin tone from flesh to rosy pink, occurs four to five weeks after conception. By then, each puppy embryo a female is carrying is little more than the size of a walnut (15–30 mm). Toward the end of the sixth week of pregnancy, the fetal skeleton is visible on abdominal radiographs.

Helpful hint: Many pug owners have their girls x-rayed at this point in order to get an idea of how many puppies to expect.

Care During Pregnancy

Some dog owners, interpreting the winking lights on their females' under-

bellies as a call to action, begin to rain down vitamins and minerals on their girls' meals. Or they begin making mountains out of the customary molehills in their females' food bowls. Such attentions are not necessary and may be counterproductive. For the first four weeks of your pug's pregnancy, groom her as usual, play with her as usual, and feed her as usual—as long as you are feeding a product that is 100 percent nutritionally complete and balanced for all stages of a dog's life. (See "How to Decipher a Dog-food Label," page 40.) If you must give your pug something extra, make it extra attention.

Begin to increase your female's rations gradually during her fifth week of pregnancy. If, for example, she normally eats ⅔ cup of dry food and 3.25 ounces (92 g) of canned food daily, she could probably use 1 to 1⅓ cups of dry and up to 6.5 ounces (184 g) of canned each day by the end of her term. Because a female's abdomen becomes crowded during pregnancy, distribute her food over three meals a day soon after you begin increasing her rations.

In addition to giving their pregnant females extra food, some owners switch from regular dry food to puppy chow when a female is about six weeks pregnant. Others switch to puppy chow as soon as a female has been mated. Whatever you and your veterinarian decide is best for your pug, be careful not to overfeed her while she is pregnant. Females that gain too much weight during pregnancy often have large puppies, poor muscle tone, fatty deposits that narrow the birth canal through which their fat puppies must pass, and deliveries made difficult by a lack of stamina.

Just as overfeeding during pregnancy is counterproductive, so are overdoses of vitamins and minerals. Excess calcium, phosphorous, and vitamin D, for example, can cause bone and kidney damage. Excess vitamin A can cause coat loss, bone deformities, and liver disease.

Finally, females should not be exposed to teratogens during pregnancy. Defined as substances that disrupt normal embryonic development, teratogens include live-virus vaccines, excess doses of vitamin A, some steroids, and griseofulvin, an antidote for ringworm. These and other teratogenic substances are always potentially harmful to the developing embryo. Indeed, pregnant females should not be given any medication unless it has been prescribed by a veterinarian.

Preparing for Delivery

Gestation, the period between conception and birth, lasts on average 63 days after the first successful mating—give or take three or four days in either direction. Puppies are not viable on average until the 57th day of gestation.

About the start of her last week of pregnancy, the female may begin to investigate open closets, drawers, and the undersides of beds in search of a nesting place. (Or you may find her, as we regularly found one of our girls, trying to burrow under the pillows on the bed while we were occupying them.) From that point on, she ought never to be left alone for more than a few minutes at a time.

Given the choice, most females would spend the last several nights of pregnancy on their owners' beds. In fact, that is where many dogs, pregnant or otherwise, prefer to spend their nights. If anyone objects to this arrangement, the female should sleep in a large crate—approximately 24 inches (60 cm) long, 36 inches (91 cm) wide, and 24 inches (60. cm) high—in her owner's bedroom. The bedroom door should be kept closed, and children and other pets should be kept at bay. With the female close at hand, even comatose sleepers will respond to any unusual noises, ratting about in the crate, or sounds of distress in the night. (Crates can be purchased from pet shops, vendors at dog shows, and from companies that advertise in dog magazines.)

Provision the female's crate with water and a whelping box. If you use a cardboard box for a nest, leave three sides intact and cut the front side down so that a 6-inch-high strip (15.2 cm) is left at the bottom to prevent newborn puppies from crawling out. Spray the nesting box with a mild, nonammonia-based disinfectant and wipe it dry before placing it in the crate. Some people use cloth towels to line the nesting box, others use newspaper or paper towels.

When their puppies are young, many pug mothers feel most secure if their whelping boxes are placed in their crates.

Delivering Puppies

Many breeders begin taking their females' temperatures morning and night with a rectal thermometer on day 58 after the first mating. A dog's normal temperature is between 100°–102.5°F (37.7°–39.1°C). If her temperature drops to 99°F (37°C) or below, puppies most likely will arrive within 12 hours, although some females deliver without exhibiting a drop in temperature, and some deliver more than 12 hours after their temperatures drop. But if the temperature rises two or three degrees above normal, call the vet at once.

Temperature is not the only sign of impending delivery. Other signs include rapid breathing, pacing, turning around in circles, frequent, somewhat anxious attention to the genital area, and loss of appetite. The more intense these signs become, the closer a female is to delivering.

A final sign that delivery is nigh is the passing of the placental plug. A gelatinous stopper that forms at the cervix early during gestation to pro- tect the uterus from external infection, the plug is expelled when the cervix begins to relax in anticipation of delivery. The clear, stringy mucus that accompanies the passing of the plug may appear a few hours or a day or two before puppies start to arrive.

As long as a female emits a clear, odorless substance, her owner need not worry; but if a dark, green-tinted, odoriferous fluid appears and it is not followed shortly by a puppy, call your veterinarian at once. More than likely a placenta has separated from the wall of the uterus and a puppy is in danger of dying from lack of oxygen— if it has not died already.

Labor begins with involuntary uterine contractions, which usually are preceded by rapid breathing and panting. Not long after involuntary contractions have begun, a female supplements them by contracting her abdominal muscles in an effort to deliver her first puppy. When abdominal contractions begin, you should note the time carefully. If the first puppy does not appear within an

Like human children lined up at an ice cream truck, these puppies have flagged their mother down for a snack.

Still life with puppy, whose legs and focus are in the wobbly stage of development.

hour, call the vet—and have a clean, towel-lined carrier ready.

As delivery begins, a dark, gray bubble emerges from the vagina. Once that bubble of new life appears, the clock should be reset to 30 minutes. If the female cannot give birth to the puppy during that time, either on her own or with help from her owner, call the veterinarian.

Puppies may present anteriorly (head first) or posteriorly (tail first). In anterior presentations, if the female does not deliver a puppy within a few minutes after its head has emerged from her vaginal opening, remove the amniotic sack (placental membrane) from around the puppy's face to prevent suffocation. The membrane should break and peel away easily if you rub the top of the puppy's skull gently with a clean finger or a piece of clean cloth. If the membrane breaks, peel it away from the puppy's face. If the membrane does not break, pinch it between your thumb and forefinger at the base of the puppy's skull and pull it away from the skull carefully. You may have to push the lips of the female's vulva back from the puppy's head in order to grasp the membrane at the base of the skull.

If another five minutes go by and the female has not delivered the puppy on her own, you may be able

The required elements of the puppy-delivery kit should be gathered several days in advance of the time when they will be needed.

The Puppy-delivery List

Be sure to have the following items assembled a few days before your female is expected to go into labor. While you are gathering the items on your puppy-delivery list, take a minute to clip your female's claws.

- the veterinarian's emergency phone number
- clean, soft cloths
- clean towels
- small hemostat (presterilized in boiling water)
- blunt scissors (presterilized in boiling water)
- baby-bulb syringe or other aspirator
- heating pad with adjustable temperature control
- rectal thermometer
- small box
- several syringes
- clean, towel-lined carrier
- sterile rubber gloves
- cotton balls or large, sterile gauze pads
- white iodine
- Vaseline
- baby oil
- styptic powder
- oxytocin (optional)
- Dopram-V (optional)
- dextrose solution (refrigerated)
- can of commercial mother's-milk replacer
- coffee

to pull it free. You also may injure the puppy in the process. Injury is best avoided if you try to ease the puppy out rather than wrench it out. After washing your hands, grasp the puppy between the thumb and forefinger of one hand as far behind the puppy's head as possible. If enough of the puppy is protruding, hook it between your index and middle fingers just behind its front legs. At the same time, support the female's abdomen with the other hand and push upward on the abdomen. Then pull the puppy gently downward. If this does not free the puppy and the female is not able to deliver it on her own within 30 minutes, call the veterinarian.

In posterior presentations, also known as breech births, time is more precious because you cannot remove the membrane from the puppy's face. What's more, if the umbilical cord is pinched inside the birth canal, cutting off the maternal blood supply to the puppy, it will suffocate. If a puppy presents posteriorly and is not delivered within five minutes, begin trying to pull it out, using the technique described above. (This time, of course, you will try to hook your fingers in front of the hind legs.) If you are not successful after 10 to 15 minutes, call your vet.

Some people try to prompt delivery by giving their females a shot of oxytocin, a pituitary hormone that helps to stimulate uterine contractions. Do not attempt this at home without discussing the possibility with your veterinarian— and learning in advance how to give a shot. Oxytocin never should be administered before a puppy is visible in the vaginal opening. A female can die of a ruptured uterus if she is given oxytocin before her cervix is fully dilated, and it is not easy for a nonprofessional to determine when dilation has occurred.

Once a puppy has been born, the mother should begin licking it vigorously to clean it and to remove the placental membrane. If she does not remove the membrane from the puppy's face at once, do it for her. Healthy puppies usually move about in search of a nipple and may begin nursing within 15 minutes after birth. In the meantime, the mother normally will try to sever the umbilical cord with her teeth once she has passed the placenta, which usually occurs 5 to 15 minutes after she has delivered the puppy. Once the placenta has been expelled, the next puppy, if there is one, should appear within 10 to 90 minutes; but the interval between births is not as important as the mother's behavior. If she strains to deliver a puppy without success for more than 30 minutes—or if a puppy appears in the vaginal opening and is not fully delivered within 30 minutes (10 to 15 minutes in the case of posterior presentations)—call the vet.

If a newborn puppy is breathing with difficulty or does not appear to be breathing at all, and the mother has not expelled the placenta, fasten a hemostat on the umbilical cord about 6 inches (15 cm) from the puppy. Grasp the cord on the side of the hemostat closer to the mother and tug gently. If the mother does not expel the placenta at once, do not waste time with it. Cut the cord with sterile scissors on the mother's side of the hemostat, remove the hemostat, dip the severed end of the cord still attached to the puppy into a bottle of white iodine, and try to revive the puppy.

 Place the puppy in a clean towel and then, holding the puppy in the towel between your hands, rub the puppy briskly to stimulate it and to help it to begin breathing. Hold the puppy in the palm of one hand, face up. Make sure the puppy's head is secure and immobile between your thumb and forefinger. Place your other palm over the puppy's abdomen with your forefinger over the puppy's heart. Holding the puppy securely in both hands at about eye level, swing your hands downward abruptly for a distance of 3 or 4 feet (.9–1.2 m). Press the rib cage over the puppy's heart with your forefinger as you do. Repeat two or three times. If the puppy does not begin breathing, hold

If a newborn puppy is breathing with difficulty, hold it securely in one hand, swing it downward about 3 or 4 feet, and press down on its rib cage over its heart as you do.

its mouth open and blow gently into it to resuscitate the puppy. If there is considerable mucous coming from the puppy's nose, remove the discharge with an aspirator.

Swing the puppy downward two or three times more, blow into its mouth, swing, blow into its mouth, and swing again until the puppy begins breathing or until it is obvious that the puppy is beyond reviving. Do not think about throwing in the towel until you have spent at least 30 minutes trying to revive the puppy.

Some breeders, if they cannot revive a puppy after five or ten minutes, dip it up to its neck into a bowl of very cool water and then into a bowl of very warm water in hope that the shock will kick-start its heart. Breeders who have discussed the matter with a veterinarian beforehand sometimes put a drop of the respiratory stimulant Dopram-V under the puppy's tongue to activate breathing at this point.

If a weak puppy begins breathing on its own, place it in a small box that has a heating pad on the bottom with a towel over the pad. The temperature in the box should be 85°F (29°C). To

Pug puppies are masters of the hairy eyeball, a sidelong glance that implies you are the walking equivalent of a rude noise.

maintain that temperature, you may have to put another towel loosely over the puppy, close the flaps of the box, and place a towel over the closed flaps. Give the puppy back to its mother when she has finished delivering her litter, but continue to monitor that puppy for the next two hours.

Some mothers chew each umbilical cord and eat every placenta compulsively, but after your female has consumed two placentas, dispose of any others, or she may develop an upset stomach or diarrhea. If the female shows little interest in umbilical cords or placentas, cut the cords five minutes or so after the placentas have been passed, sterilize the severed ends of the cords still attached to the puppies, and dispose of the afterbirths. (The cord should be cut about three inches from the puppy's abdomen.) Be sure all placentas are present and accounted for. A retained placenta can cause serious infection, may have to be removed surgically, and could mean that you instead of your female will be raising the litter.

After the last puppy has been delivered, the female will heave a sigh of relief and settle in to nursing and fussing over her brood. As she does, inspect each puppy for signs of abnormalities such as cleft palates and umbilical hernias.

At this point, some breeders give their females a shot of oxytocin to expel any placental debris retained during delivery. Check with your veterinarian in advance about the advisability of doing this.

Monitor the puppies and their mother for two hours after the last puppy has been born to make sure that all puppies are nursing normally and that the temperature in the puppy box is sufficient to prevent chilling. Puppies should begin nursing no later than two hours after they have been born. If a puppy appears too weak to nurse, you may have to tube feed it (see "Supplemental Feeding," page 89).

Helpful hint: Maintain the temperature in the whelping box at 85°F (29°C) by putting a heating pad under the towel in the box if necessary. Puppies' homeostatic mechanisms, which regulate their body temperature, are not completely functional at birth. Normally an attentive female's body heat will maintain puppies' temperatures at the normal 97° to 100°F (36°–37.7°C). After two weeks, the temperature in the nesting box can be reduced to 80°F (26.7°C).

Neonatal Puppy Development

Puppies should begin nursing within two hours after being born. They nurse almost hourly for the first day or two. Indeed, they have only two primary modes, nursing and sleeping, which they execute in a 1:3 ratio.

On average, pug puppies weigh between six and nine ounces (170 to 255 g) at birth, although some may weigh a little more or a little less. They may not gain weight during their first 24 hours. They may even lose a few grams. After that, however, they should gain 7 to 10 percent of their body weight each day for the first two weeks. If a puppy fails to gain weight during any 48-hour period in its first two weeks of life, or if a puppy begins to lose weight, call your veterinarian. By the time it is a month old, the average pug puppy should weigh about two pounds (.9 kg).

To support this growth, lactating females require prodigious amounts of food, two to three times as much as they would eat normally. It is virtually impossible to overfeed at this point, so give your girl as much as she wants to eat three or even four times a day. And just to be sure she is getting enough nutrients, feed her puppy chow instead of regular dry food.

Supplemental Feeding

If a puppy is not nursing, if it seems to be crying more than it is nursing, or if it is not gaining weight as it should be, it most likely will benefit from supplemental feeding. Begin by taking the puppy's temperature with a rectal thermometer that has been lubricated with Vaseline or K-Y Jelly. If the puppy's temperature is below 97°F (36°C), feed it 2 cc's of dextrose solution that has been warmed to 98°F (36.7°C). When a puppy's temperature falls below 97°F (36°C), enzymes in the puppy's stomach are not functioning well enough to digest milk.

Puppies develop a preference for an individual nipple when they are quite young. They retain that preference through puppyhood.

If the puppy's temperature is above 97°F (36°C), feed it 2 cc's of mother's milk replacer. You can obtain the dextrose solution, the mother's milk replacer, and the syringe with which to administer them from your vet a few days before your female is due. Keep the dextrose solution and the milk replacer, once it has been opened, in the refrigerator.

Whether you feed dextrose or milk, the technique is the same. Put a towel on your lap, hold the puppy in one hand, spine side up, at a 45-degree angle to your lap, slide the end of the syringe gently between the puppy's lips, and push the plunger on the syringe a fraction of an inch to release some of the contents of the syringe into the puppy's mouth. Go slowly, pushing intermittently on the plunger as the puppy sucks on the syringe. If the puppy is sucking avidly and then turns its head away, it is probably full.

Puppies that are not thriving may need supplemental feeding, which is done most easily with a syringe.

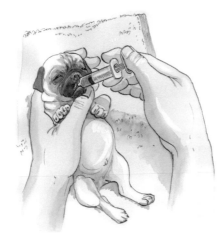

Puppies whose temperatures are normal can be returned to their mothers after supplemental feeding, but they should be monitored carefully to be sure they are nursing adequately within an hour or so. If they are not, continue supplemental feeding every two hours around the clock until they begin nursing on their own.

Puppies whose temperatures are subnormal should be placed in an incubator and monitored every hour. As long as their temperatures remain below 97°F (36°C), keep feeding the dextrose solution. When the puppy's temperature rises above 97°F (36°C), feed it a milk replacer, then give it back to its mother. Watch the puppy every hour or so to see if it is nursing properly. If not, feed it 2 cc's of dextrose solution or milk replacer every two hours around the clock until it is able to nurse normally.

Puppies too weak to suck dextrose solution or milk from a syringe may have to be tube fed. Ask your veterinarian in advance to show you how to measure the length of tube, attached to a syringe, that needs to be inserted into the puppy's stomach.

Tube feeding, if not done properly, can cause lesions of the pharynx or stomach. If the tube is inserted incorrectly and food is introduced into the lungs, the puppy may choke and die. This method of feeding should be attempted, therefore, only as a last resort.

Raising Orphaned Puppies

As we noted earlier, pugs come equipped with their own motto, *multum in parvo,* which means "a lot of dog in a small space." Some pugs—our female, Debbie, among them—believe *multum in parvo* also means their owners handle the *multum* part of raising puppies while the mothers do as *parvo* as possible. Other pugs may not be able to care for their puppies because they (the mothers) have contracted an illness or have not recovered sufficiently from a cesarean section to assume their maternal duties. In such circumstances, the owner also must be prepared to hand-raise the litter until the female recovers or the litter is old enough to eat on its own.

Orphaned puppies should be kept in an incubator at 85°F (29°C). Their temperatures should be checked every two hours around the clock for the first two or three days, and they should be fed ½ to 1 cc of warmed dextrose solution or milk replacer per ounce of body weight as their temperatures indicate.

If the puppies' temperatures are normal for a few days, you need not continue to take their temperatures before feeding. Intervals between feedings may be stretched to two and half hours during the second week. During the third and fourth weeks, feed every three hours and give the puppies all the milk they want.

Toward the end of the puppies' third week, you should begin to wean them onto solid food. Begin with a porridge of baby cereal and milk replacer for a few days, then gradually add dry puppy food that has been reduced to powder in a blender. At about four and a half or five weeks, switch to a mixture of canned puppy food and whole dry puppy food that has been soaked in milk. Finally, at about six weeks, substitute water for milk when you soak the puppies' food.

At first you will have to stimulate puppies to eliminate before feeding them because puppies do not eliminate spontaneously until they are about three weeks old. Dip a section of wadded-up paper towel into a small bowl of warm water and rub each puppy's anogenital area softly. Wash the area with a clean paper towel after the puppy eliminates and then pat the puppy dry.

Because hand-raised puppies have not received maternal antibodies, ask your veterinarian if they should be vaccinated at eight weeks or if he or she recommends starting vaccinations, using killed vaccine, when the puppies are three to four weeks old.

If hand-raising puppies sounds like work, it is. During several sleep-deprived weeks your determination and self-discipline are all that stand between life and death for the puppies. But you decided to bring them

into the world, and you are darn well responsible for seeing them through it.

When you have hand-raised a litter successfully, the puppies' progress is a bountiful reward. What's more, the puppies you have nurtured faithfully will be among the best socialized, most people-oriented tykes you will ever see.

Useful Addresses and Literature

International Kennel Clubs

American Kennel Club
   51 Madison Avenue
   New York, NY 10038
   212-696-8200

For registration information contact:
   American Kennel Club
   5580 Centerview Drive
   Raleigh, NC 27606
   919-233-9767

Australian National Kennel Council
   Royal Showgrounds
   Ascot Vale 3032
   Victoria, Australia

Canadian Kennel Club
   89 Skyway Avenue, Unit 100
   Etobicoke, Ontario
   Canada M9W 6R4
   416-675-5511

The Kennel Club
   1–5 Clargis Street
   Picadilly, London W1Y 8AB
   England

New Zealand Kennel Club
   Private Bag 50903
   Porirua
   Wellington
   New Zealand

National Breed Club

Pug Dog Club of America*
   James P. Cavallaro, Secretary
   1820 Shadowlawn Street
   Jacksonville, FL 32205-9430
   904-389-2921

*Mr. Cavallaro's term expires at the end of 1995. To obtain the names and addresses of PDCA secretaries in the future, inquire at the American Kennel Club (see phone number above).

Periodicals

Pug Talk
   223 W. Louisiana Avenue
   Dallas, TX 75224–2299
   Subscription rate: $30/year
   for six issues

Dog Fancy
   P.O. Box 53264
   Boulder, CO 80322
   303-786-7306

Dog World
   29 North Wacker Drive
   Chicago, IL 60606
   312-726-2802

National Lost-Pet Registries

Tattoo-based Registries:

National Dog Registry
   P.O. Box 118
   Woodstock, NY 12498-0116
   800-637-3647

Tattoo-A-Pet
   1625 Emmons Avenue
   Brooklyn, NY 11235
   800-TATTOOS (828-8667) or
   800-828-8007

I.D. PET
   74 Hoyt Street
   Darien, CT 06820
   800-243-9147

Centralized Tattoo Registry Information
   15870 Allen Road
   Taylor, MI 48180
   313-285-6311

Microchip-based Registry:

Info Pet Identification Systems
   517 W. Travelers Trail
   Minneapolis, MN 55337
   800-INFOPET (463-6738)

No Tattoo or Microchip Required:

Petfinders
   368 High Street
   Athol, New York 12810
   800-223-4747

Animal Protection Organizations

American Humane Association
   P.O. Box 1266
   Denver, CO 80201
   303-695-0811

American Society for the Prevention of Cruelty to Animals
   441 East 92nd Street
   New York, NY 10128
   212-876-7700

Friends of Animals
   P.O. Box 1244
   Norwalk, CT 06856
   For information about FoA's low-cost, neutering-and-spaying program call:
   800-631-2212

The Fund for Animals
   200 W. 57th Street
   New York, NY 10019
   212-246-2096

The Humane Society of the United States
   2100 L Street, NW
   Washington, D.C. 20037
   202-452-1100

Further Reading

Alderton, David, *The Dog Care Manual,* Barron's Educational Series, Inc., Hauppauge, New York, 1986.

Barish, Eileen, *Vacationing with Your Pet!,* Pet-Friendly Publications, Scottsdale, Arizona, 1994.

Baer, Ted, *Communicating with Your Dog,* Barron's Educational Series, Inc., Hauppauge, New York, 1989.

Carlson, Delbert G., D.V.M., and Griffin, James M., M.D., *Dog Owner's Home Veterinary Handbook,* Howell Book House, New York, 1980.

Fogle, Bruce, D.V.M., M.R.C.V.S., *The Dog's Mind: Understanding Your Dog's Behavior,* Howell Book House, New York, 1990.

Frye, Fredric, *First Aid for Your Dog,* Barron's Educational Series, Inc., Hauppauge, New York, 1987.

Gore, Louise V. and Heathman, Marcy, *Meet the Pug for Years of Happiness,* Doral Publishing, Wilsonville, Oregon, 1990.

Klever, Ulrich, *The Complete Book of Dog Care,* Barron's Educational Series, Inc., Hauppauge, New York, 1989.

Pinney, Chris C., *Guide to Home Pet Grooming,* Barron's Educational Series, Inc., Hauppauge, New York, 1990.

Thomas, Shirley, *The New Pug,* Howell Book House, New York, 1990.

Wrede, Barbara, *Civilizing Your Puppy,* Barron's Educational Series, Inc., Hauppauge, New York, 1992.

Acknowledgments

Several people provided suggestions, encouragement, and support in the preparation of this book. Charlotte and Edward Patterson, our pug mentors and, more important, our good friends, reviewed several parts of the manuscript. Their help with the chapter "Two for the Shows" was especially valuable. They saved me from public embarrassment regarding show rules, classes, and related matters in the portions of that chapter they reviewed. I should like to return the favor by indemnifying them from responsibility for any errors of fact that might remain in the portions of that chapter they did not review.

Nancy J. Nelson, V.M.D., reviewed the chapter "Whelping and Raising Puppies." In addition to the help she provided with the delivery of that chapter, she also delivered the first two puppies in a litter of six that were born last December 30.

David A. Dzanis, D.V.M., Ph.D., a veterinary nutritionist for the Food and Drug Administration, was an invaluable help with the chapter "The Well-fed Pug." He provided information for that chapter, in addition to explaining, patiently and clearly, certain nutritional concepts and the meanings of a number of long words.

Don Reis, senior editor at Barron's, was a gentleman, scholar, and judge of fine writing, as always. Don does what all great editors do: he makes everyone else on the team look better.

The four adult pug dogs who live in our house—Percy, Debbie, Patty, and Ella—supplied soothing background snoring when I was working, heads to scratch while I was waiting for the muse, and an ever ready excuse to go cruising in the van when I really should have been working. Patty, who belongs to the Pattersons, also supplied a litter of six puppies. Hans, the newest pug member of Clan Maggitti, was too busy learning to walk, to elbow his littermates away from the food bowls, and to engage in the slam dancing that is all puppies' delight to be much help with this book, but his turn will come.

Of course, the greatest help in writing this or any book is the companionship of someone who shares your enthusiasm for a subject and whose observations about that subject invariably make you think, "I've got to use that in the book." I am grateful to my wife Mary Ann for making those observations.

About the Author

Phil Maggitti is a freelance writer and editor who lives in southeastern Pennsylvania with his wife Mary Ann, five pug dogs, and ten cats. His writing to date has concentrated on the points at which the lives of people and animals intersect. He has written more than 450 articles describing those intersections, in addition to his nonanimal-related work. He also has written several books, including two for Barron's Educational Series: *Scottish Fold Cats* and *Guide to a Well-behaved Cat: A Sound Approach to Cat Training.*

Important Notes

This pet owner's guide tells the reader how to buy and care for a pug. The author and the publisher consider it important to point out that the advice given in the book is meant primarily for normally developed puppies from a good breeder—that is, dogs of excellent physical health and good character.

Anyone who adopts a fully grown dog should be aware that the animal has already formed its basic impressions of human beings. The new owner should watch the animal carefully, including its behavior towards humans, and should meet the previous owner. If the dog comes from a shelter, it may be possible to get some information on the dog's background and peculiarities there. There are dogs that as a result of bad experiences with humans behave in an unnatural manner or may even bite. Only people that have experience with dogs should take in such an animal.

Caution is further advised in the association of children with dogs, in meetings with other dogs, and in exercising the dog without a leash.

Even well-behaved and carefully supervised dogs sometimes do damage to someone else's property or cause accidents. It is therefore in the owner's interest to be adequately insured against such eventualities, and we strongly urge all dog owners to purchase a liability policy that covers their dog.

Photo Credits

Susan Green: pages 9 (lower), 13 (lower), 19 (right), 33 (upper left), 45, 68, 69, 80, back cover.
Aaron Norman: pages 5, 48, 58, 63, 65 (lower).
Bob Schwartz: front cover, inside front cover, inside back cover, pages 8, 9 (upper), 12, 13 (upper), 16 (two), 18, 19 (left), 23, 26, 27, 31, 33 (two), 37, 41, 55, 65 (upper), 72, 81, 84, 85, 88, 89.
Judith Strom: pages 59, 73.

All inquiries should be addressed to
Barron's Educational Series, Inc.
250 Wireless Boulevard
Hauppauge, NY 11788

International Standard Book No. 0-8120-1824-9

Library of Congress Catalog No. 94-20410

Library of Congress Cataloging-in-Publication Data
Maggitti, Phil.
    Pugs : everything about purchase, care, nutrition, breeding, behavior, and training / Phil Maggitti ; drawings by Michele Earle-Bridges.
        p.   cm.
    Includes bibliographical references (p. 92) and index.
        ISBN 0-8120-1824-9
        1. Pug. I. Title.
SF429.P9M34   1994
636.7´6—dc20   94-20410
                                                      CIP

PRINTED IN HONG KONG

45678   9927   987654321

Index

Color photos are indicated in **boldface** type.

Perfect for Pet Owners!

PET OWNER'S MANUALS

Over 50 illustrations per book (20 or more color photos), 72–80 pp., paperback.

AFRICAN GRAY PARROTS (3773-1)
AMAZON PARROTS (4035-X)
BANTAMS (3687-5)
BEAGLES (3829-0)
BEEKEEPING (4089-9)
BOSTON TERRIERS (1696-3)
BOXERS (4036-8)
CANARIES (4611-0)
CATS (4442-8)
CHINCHILLAS (4037-6)
CHOW-CHOWS (3952-1)
CICHLIDS (4597-1)
COCKATIELS (4610-2)
COCKATOOS (4159-3)
CONURES (4880-6)
DACHSHUNDS (1843-5)
DALMATIANS (4605-6)
DISCUS FISH (4669-2)
DOBERMAN PINSCHERS (2999-2)
DOGS (4822-9)
DWARF RABBITS (1352-2)
ENGLISH SPRINGER SPANIELS (1778-1)
FEEDING AND SHELTERING BACKYARD BIRDS (4252-2)
FEEDING AND SHELTERING EUROPEAN BIRDS (2858-9)
FERRETS (2976-3)
GERBILS (3725-1)
GERMAN SHEPHERDS (2982-8)
GOLDEN RETRIEVERS (3793-6)
GOLDFISH (2975-5)
GOULDIAN FINCHES (4523-8)
GUINEA PIGS (4612-9)
HAMSTERS (4439-8)
IRISH SETTERS (4663-3)
KEESHONDEN (1560-6)
KILLIFISH (4475-4)
LABRADOR RETRIEVERS (3792-8)
LHASA APSOS (3950-5)
LIZARDS IN THE TERRARIUM (3925-4)
LONGHAIRED CATS (2803-1)
LONG-TAILED PARAKEETS (1351-4)
LORIES AND LORIKEETS (1567-3)
LOVEBIRDS (3726-X)

MACAWS (4768-0)
MICE (2921-6)
MINIATURE PIGS (1356-5)
MUTTS (4126-7)
MYNAHS (3688-3)
PARAKEETS (4437-1)
PARROTS (4823-7)
PERSIAN CATS (4405-3)
PIGEONS (4044-9)
POMERANIANS (4670-6)
PONIES (2856-2)
POODLES (2812-0)
RABBITS (4440-1)
RATS (4535-1)
ROTTWEILERS (4483-5)
SCHNAUZERS (3949-1)
SHAR-PEI (4334-2)
SHEEP (4091-0)
SHETLAND SHEEPDOGS (4264-6)
SHIH TZUS (4524-6)
SIAMESE CATS (4764-8)
SIBERIAN HUSKIES (4265-4)
SNAKES (2813-9)
SPANIELS (2424-9)
TROPICAL FISH (4700-1)
TURTLES (4702-8)
YORKSHIRE TERRIERS (4406-1)
ZEBRA FINCHES (3497-X)

NEW PET HANDBOOKS

Detailed, illustrated profiles (40–60 color photos), 144 pp., paperback.

NEW AQUARIUM FISH HANDBOOK (3682-4)
NEW AUSTRALIAN PARAKEET HANDBOOK (4739-7)
NEW BIRD HANDBOOK (4157-7)
NEW CANARY HANDBOOK (4879-2)
NEW CAT HANDBOOK (2922-4)
NEW COCKATIEL HANDBOOK (4201-8)
NEW DOG HANDBOOK (2857-0)
NEW DUCK HANDBOOK (4088-0)
NEW FINCH HANDBOOK (2859-7)
NEW GOAT HANDBOOK (4090-2)
NEW PARAKEET HANDBOOK (2985-2)
NEW PARROT HANDBOOK (3729-4)
NEW RABBIT HANDBOOK (4202-6)

NEW SALTWATER AQUARIUM HANDBOOK (4482-7)
NEW SOFTBILL HANDBOOK (4075-9)
NEW TERRIER HANDBOOK (3951-3)

REFERENCE BOOKS

Comprehensive, lavishly illustrated references (60–300 color photos), 136–176 pp., hardcover & paperback.

AQUARIUM FISH (1350-6)
AQUARIUM FISH BREEDING (4474-6)
AQUARIUM FISH SURVIVAL MANUAL (5686-8)
AQUARIUM PLANTS MANUAL (1687-4)
BEFORE YOU BUY THAT PUPPY (1750-1)
BEST PET NAME BOOK EVER, THE (4258-1)
CARING FOR YOUR SICK CAT (1726-9)
CAT CARE MANUAL (5765-1)
CIVILIZING YOUR PUPPY (4953-5)
COMMUNICATING WITH YOUR DOG (4203-4)
COMPLETE BOOK OF BUDGERIGARS (6059-8)
COMPLETE BOOK OF CAT CARE (4613-7)
COMPLETE BOOK OF DOG CARE (4158-5)
COMPLETE BOOK OF PARROTS (5971-9)
DOG CARE MANUAL (5764-3)
FEEDING YOUR PET BIRD (1521-3)
GOLDFISH AND ORNAMENTAL CARP (5634-5)
GUIDE TO A WELL BEHAVED CAT (1476-6)
GUIDE TO HOME PET GROOMING (4298-0)
HEALTHY DOG, HAPPY DOG (1842-7)
HOP TO IT: A Guide to Training Your Pet Rabbit (4551-3)
HORSE CARE MANUAL (5795-3)
HOW TO TALK TO YOUR CAT (1749-8)
HOW TO TEACH YOUR OLD DOG NEW TRICKS (4544-0)
LABYRINTH FISH (5635-3)
MACAWS (6073-3)
NONVENOMOUS SNAKES (5632-9)
WATER PLANTS IN THE AQUARIUM (3926-2)

Barron's Educational Series, Inc. • 250 Wireless Blvd., Hauppauge, NY 11788
Call toll-free: 1-800-645-3476 • In Canada: Georgetown Book Warehouse
34 Armstrong Ave., Georgetown, Ont. L7G 4R9 • Call toll-free: 1-800-247-7160
ISBN prefix: 0-8120 • Order from your favorite book or pet store